MznLnx

Missing Links Exam Preps

Exam Prep for

Managerial Economics: Applications, Strategies, and Tactics

McGuigan, Moyer & Harris, 11th Edition

The MznLnx Exam Prep is your link from the texbook and lecture to your exams.
The MznLnx Exam Preps are unauthorized and comprehensive reviews of your textbooks.

All material provided by MznLnx and Rico Publications (c) 2010
Textbook publishers and textbook authors do not particpate in or contribute to these reviews.

MznLnx

Rico
Publications

Exam Prep for Managerial Economics: Applications, Strategies, and Tactics
11th Edition
McGuigan, Moyer & Harris

Publisher: Raymond Houge
Assistant Editor: Michael Rouger
Text and Cover Designer: Lisa Buckner
Marketing Manager: Sara Swagger
Project Manager, Editorial Production: Jerry Emerson
Art Director: Vernon Lowerui

Product Manager: Dave Mason
Editorial Assitant: Rachel Guzmanji
Pedagogy: Debra Long
Cover Image: Jim Reed/Getty Images
Text and Cover Printer: City Printing, Inc.
Compositor: Media Mix, Inc.

(c) 2010 Rico Publications

ALL RIGHTS RESERVED. No part of this work covered by the copyright may be reproduced or used in any form or by an means--graphic, electronic, or mechanical, including photocopying, recording, taping, Web distribution, information storage, and retrieval systems, or in any other manner--without the written permission of the publisher.

For more information about our products, contact us at:

Dave.Mason@RicoPublications.com

For permission to use material from this text or product, submit a request online to:

Dave.Mason@RicoPublications.com

Printed in the United States
ISBN:

Contents

CHAPTER 1
Introduction and Goals of the Firm — 1

CHAPTER 2
Fundamental Economic Concepts — 8

CHAPTER 3
Demand Analysis — 21

CHAPTER 4
Estimating Demand — 26

CHAPTER 5
Business and Economic Forecasting — 31

CHAPTER 6
Managing Exports — 36

CHAPTER 7
Production Economics — 48

CHAPTER 8
Cost Analysis — 55

CHAPTER 9
Applications of Cost Theory — 62

CHAPTER 10
Prices, Output, and Strategy: Pure and Monopolistic Competition — 65

CHAPTER 11
Price and Output Determination: Monopoly and Dominant Firms — 72

CHAPTER 12
Price and Output Determination: Oligopoly — 79

CHAPTER 13
Best-Practice Tactics: Game Theory — 83

CHAPTER 14
Pricing Techniques and Analysis — 92

CHAPTER 15
Contracting, Governance, and Organizational Form — 99

CHAPTER 16
Government Regulation — 108

CHAPTER 17
Long-Term Investment Analysis — 116

ANSWER KEY — 126

TO THE STUDENT

COMPREHENSIVE

The *MznLnx* Exam Prep series is designed to help you pass your exams. Editors at MznLnx review your textbooks and then prepare these practice exams to help you master the textbook material. Unlike study guides, workbooks, and practice tests provided by the texbook publisher and textbook authors, *MznLnx* gives you **all** of the material in each chapter in exam form, not just samples, so you can be sure to nail your exam.

MECHANICAL

The MznLnx Exam Prep series creates exams that will help you learn the subject matter as well as test you on your understanding. Each question is designed to help you master the concept. Just working through the exams, you gain an understanding of the subject--its a simple mechanical process that produces success.

INTEGRATED STUDY GUIDE AND REVIEW

MznLnx is not just a set of exams designed to test you, its also a comprehensive review of the subject content. Each exam question is also a review of the concept, making sure that you will get the answer correct without having to go to other sources of material. You learn as you go! Its the easiest way to pass an exam.

HUMOR

Studying can be tedious and dry. MznLnx's instructional design includes moderate humor within the exam questions on occassion, to break the tedium and revitalize the brain

Chapter 1. Introduction and Goals of the Firm

1. _____s is the social science that studies the production, distribution, and consumption of goods and services. The term _____s comes from the Ancient Greek οἰκονομία from οἶκος (oikos, 'house') + νόμος (nomos, 'custom' or 'law'), hence 'rules of the house(hold)'. Current _____ models developed out of the broader field of political economy in the late 19th century, owing to a desire to use an empirical approach more akin to the physical sciences.
   a. Inflation
   b. Energy economics
   c. Opportunity cost
   d. Economic

2. _____, is a branch of economics that applies microeconomic analysis to decision methods of businesses or other management units. As such, it bridges economic theory and economics in practice. It draws heavily from quantitative techniques such as regression analysis and correlation, Lagrangian calculus (linear.)
   a. Black-Litterman model
   b. Forward exchange market
   c. Managerial economics
   d. Club goods

3. In economics, _____ is the difference between a company's total revenue and its opportunity costs. It is the increase in wealth that an investor has from making an investment, taking into consideration all costs associated with that investment including the opportunity cost of capital.

Profit is the factor income of the entrepreneur.

   a. Accounting profit
   b. Economic profit
   c. ACCRA Cost of Living Index
   d. Operating profit

4. In economics, a _____ exists when a specific individual or enterprise has sufficient control over a particular product or service to determine significantly the terms on which other individuals shall have access to it. Monopolies are thus characterized by a lack of economic competition for the good or service that they provide and a lack of viable substitute goods. The verb 'monopolize' refers to the process by which a firm gains persistently greater market share than what is expected under perfect competition.
   a. 1921 recession
   b. 100-year flood
   c. 130-30 fund
   d. Monopoly

5. A mutual _____ or stockholder is an individual or company (including a corporation) that legally owns one or more shares of stock in a joint stock company. A company's _____s collectively own that company. Thus, the typical goal of such companies is to enhance _____ value.
   a. Relative valuation
   b. Prime Standard
   c. Profit warning
   d. Shareholder

6. _____ is used to assign the available resources in an economic way. It is part of resource management.

In strategic planning,is a plan for using available resources, for example human resources, especially in the near term, to achieve goals for the future.

   a. 130-30 fund
   b. 100-year flood
   c. 1921 recession
   d. Resource allocation

7. In algebra, a _____ is a function depending on n that associates a scalar, det(A), to an n×n square matrix A. The fundamental geometric meaning of a _____ is a scale factor for measure when A is regarded as a linear transformation. _____s are important both in calculus, where they enter the substitution rule for several variables, and in multilinear algebra.

For a fixed nonnegative integer n, there is a unique _____ function for the n×n matrices over any commutative ring R. In particular, this function exists when R is the field of real or complex numbers.

   a. 100-year flood
   b. Determinant
   c. 1921 recession
   d. 130-30 fund

8. _____ is the a method of technical and economic research of the systems for purpose to optimize a parity between system's consumer functions or properties and expenses to achieve those functions or properties.

Chapter 1. Introduction and Goals of the Firm

This methodology for continuous perfection of production, industrial technologies, organizational structures was developed by Juryj Sobolev in 1948 at the 'Perm telephone factory'

- 1948 Juryj Sobolev - the first success in application of a method analysis at the 'Perm telephone factory'.
- 1949 - the first application for the invention as result of use of the new method.

Today in economically developed countries practically each enterprise or the company use methodology of the kind of functional-cost analysis as a practice of the quality management, most full satisfying to principles of standards of series ISO 9000.

- Interest of consumer not in products itself, but the advantage which it will receive from its usage.
- The consumer aspires to reduce his expenses
- Functions needed by consumer can be executed in the various ways, and, hence, with various efficiency and expenses. Among possible alternatives of realization of functions exist such in which the parity of quality and the price is the optimal for the consumer.

The goal of _____ is achievement of the highest consumer satisfaction of production at simultaneous decrease in all kinds of industrial expenses Classical _____ has three English synonyms - Value Engineering, Value Management, Value Analysis.

a. Monopoly wage
b. Willingness to pay
c. Staple financing
d. Function cost analysis

9. _____ is the difference between price and the costs of bringing to market whatever it is that is accounted as an enterprise (whether by harvest, extraction, manufacture, or purchase) in terms of the component costs of delivered goods and/or services and any operating or other expenses.

A key difficulty in measuring profit is in defining costs. Pure economic monetary profits can be zero or negative even in competitive equilibrium when accounted monetized costs exceed monetized price.

a. Economic profit
b. Operating profit
c. ACCRA Cost of Living Index
d. Accounting profit

10. In political science and economics, the _____ or agency dilemma treats the difficulties that arise under conditions of incomplete and asymmetric information when a principal hires an agent, such as the problem that the two may not have the same interests, while the principal is, presumably, hiring the agent to pursue the interests of the former.

Various mechanisms may be used to try to align the interests of the agent with those of the principal, such as piece rates/commissions, profit sharing, efficiency wages, performance measurement (including financial statements), the agent posting a bond, or fear of firing. The _____ is found in most employer/employee relationships, for example, when stockholders hire top executives of corporations.

a. 1921 recession
b. Principal-agent problem
c. 100-year flood
d. 130-30 fund

11. _____ refers to the movement of cash into or out of a business or financial product. It is usually measured during a specified, finite period of time. Measurement of _____ can be used

- to determine a project's rate of return or value. The time of _____s into and out of projects are used as inputs in financial models such as internal rate of return, and net present value.
- to determine problems with a business's liquidity. Being profitable does not necessarily mean being liquid. A company can fail because of a shortage of cash, even while profitable.
- as an alternate measure of a business's profits when it is believed that accrual accounting concepts do not represent economic realities. For example, a company may be notionally profitable but generating little operational cash (as may be the case for a company that barters its products rather than selling for cash.) In such a case, the company may be deriving additional operating cash by issuing shares evaluating default risk, re-investment requirements, etc.

_____ is a generic term used differently depending on the context. It may be defined by users for their own purposes.

a. Strip financing
b. Restricted stock
c. Second lien loan
d. Cash flow

12. An _____ is an economic concept that relates to the cost incurred by an entity (such as organizations) associated with problems such as divergent management-shareholder objectives and information asymmetry. The costs consist of two main sources:

1. The costs inherently associated with using an agent (e.g., the risk that agents will use organizational resource for their own benefit) and
2. The costs of techniques used to mitigate the problems associated with using an agent (e.g., the costs of producing financial statements or the use of stock options to align executive interests to shareholder interests.)

Though effects of _____ are present in any agency relationship, the term is most used in business contexts.

Chapter 1. Introduction and Goals of the Firm 5

The information asymmetry that exists between shareholders and the Chief Executive Officer is generally considered to be a classic example of a principal-agent problem. The agent (the manager) is working on behalf of the principal (the shareholders), who does not observe the actions of the agent.

   a. Agency cost
   b. AD-IA Model
   c. ACCRA Cost of Living Index
   d. ACEA agreement

13. _____ is the corporate management term for the act of reorganizing the legal, ownership, operational or better organized for its present needs. Alternate reasons for restructing include a change of ownership or ownership structure, demerger repositioning debt _____ and financial _____.
   a. Market value
   b. Restructuring
   c. Securitization
   d. Forecast period

14. _____ relates to decisions that define expectations, grant power, or verify performance. It consists either of a separate process or of a specific part of management or leadership processes. Sometimes people set up a government to administer these processes and systems.
   a. 130-30 fund
   b. 1921 recession
   c. Governance
   d. 100-year flood

15. _____ is the prospect that a party insulated from risk may behave differently from the way it would behave if it were fully exposed to the risk. In insurance, _____ that occurs without conscious or malicious action is called morale hazard.

_____ is related to information asymmetry, a situation in which one party in a transaction has more information than another.

   a. Moral hazard
   b. 130-30 fund
   c. 100-year flood
   d. 1921 recession

16. In economics, the _____ is the agent who receives the net income (income after deducting all costs.)

Residual claimancy is generally required in order for there to be Moral Hazard, which is a problem typical of information asymmetry. This is specifically the case for the Principal-agent problem.

a. Free contract
b. Horizontal merger
c. Frontier markets
d. Residual claimant

17. The _____ is the part of economic and administrative life that deals with the delivery of goods and services by and for the government, whether national, regional or local/municipal.

Examples of _____ activity range from delivering social security, administering urban planning and organising national defenses.

The organization of the _____ can take several forms, including:

- Direct administration funded through taxation; the delivering organization generally has no specific requirement to meet commercial success criteria, and production decisions are determined by government.
- Publicly owned corporations (in some contexts, especially manufacturing, 'state-owned enterprises'); which differ from direct administration in that they have greater commercial freedoms and are expected to operate according to commercial criteria, and production decisions are not generally taken by government (although goals may be set for them by government.)
- Partial outsourcing (of the scale many businesses do, e.g. for IT services), is considered a _____ model.

A borderline form is

- Complete outsourcing or contracting out, with a privately owned corporation delivering the entire service on behalf of government. This may be considered a mixture of private sector operations with public ownership of assets, although in some forms the private sector's control and/or risk is so great that the service may no longer be considered part of the _____.

a. 130-30 fund
b. 100-year flood
c. Public sector
d. Policy cycle

Chapter 1. Introduction and Goals of the Firm 7

18. _____ is a term that refers both to:

- a formal discipline used to help appraise, or assess, the case for a project or proposal, which itself is a process known as project appraisal; and
- an informal approach to making decisions of any kind.

Under both definitions the process involves, whether explicitly or implicitly, weighing the total expected costs against the total expected benefits of one or more actions in order to choose the best or most profitable option. The formal process is often referred to as either CBA (_____) or BCost-benefit analysis

A hallmark of CBA is that all benefits and all costs are expressed in money terms, and are adjusted for the time value of money, so that all flows of benefits and flows of project costs over time (which tend to occur at different points in time) are expressed on a common basis in terms of their e;present value.e; Closely related, but slightly different, formal techniques include Cost-effectiveness analysis, Economic impact analysis, Fiscal impact analysis and Social Return on Investment(SROI) analysis. The latter builds upon the logic of _____, but differs in that it is explicitly designed to inform the practical decision-making of enterprise managers and investors focused on optimising their social and environmental impacts.

   a. 130-30 fund
   b. 100-year flood
   c. Decision theory
   d. Cost-benefit analysis

19. In economics, a _____ is a good that is non-rivaled and non-excludable. This means, respectively, that consumption of the good by one individual does not reduce availability of the good for consumption by others; and that no one can be effectively excluded from using the good. In the real world, there may be no such thing as an absolutely non-rivaled and non-excludable good; but economists think that some goods approximate the concept closely enough for the analysis to be economically useful.
   a. Demand-pull theory
   b. Happiness economics
   c. Neoclassical synthesis
   d. Public good

20. A _____ is an object whose consumption increases the utility of the consumer, for which the quantity demanded exceeds the quantity supplied at zero price. _____s are usually modeled as having diminishing marginal utility. The first individual purchase has high utility; the second has less.
   a. Good
   b. Merit good
   c. Composite good
   d. Pie method

Chapter 2. Fundamental Economic Concepts

1. _____s is the social science that studies the production, distribution, and consumption of goods and services. The term _____s comes from the Ancient Greek oá¼°κονομῑα from oá¼¶κος (oikos, 'house') + vÏŒμος (nomos, 'custom' or 'law'), hence 'rules of the house(hold)'. Current _____ models developed out of the broader field of political economy in the late 19th century, owing to a desire to use an empirical approach more akin to the physical sciences.
    a. Energy economics
    b. Inflation
    c. Opportunity cost
    d. Economic

2. _____ is the process of understanding, anticipating and influencing consumer behavior in order to maximize revenue or profits from a fixed, perishable resource This process was first discovered by Dr. Matt H. Keller. The challenge is to sell the right resources to the right customer at the right time for the right price.
    a. Subscription
    b. Freebie marketing
    c. Coopetition
    d. Yield management

3. Economics:

    - _____,the desire to own something and the ability to pay for it
    - _____ curve,a graphic representation of a _____ schedule
    - _____ deposit, the money in checking accounts
    - _____ pull theory,the theory that inflation occurs when _____ for goods and services exceeds existing supplies
    - _____ schedule,a table that lists the quantity of a good a person will buy it each different price
    - _____ side economics,the school of economics at believes government spending and tax cuts open economy by raising _____

    a. Production
    b. Variability
    c. Demand
    d. McKesson ' Robbins scandal

4. _____ is an economic concept with commonplace familiarity. It is the price that a good or service is offered at, or will fetch, in the marketplace. It is of interest mainly in the study of microeconomics.

Chapter 2. Fundamental Economic Concepts

a. Paper trading
b. Market anomaly
c. Noisy market hypothesis
d. Market price

5. _____ is an economic model based on price, utility and quantity in a market. It predicts that in a competitive market, price will function to equalize the quantity demanded by consumers, and the quantity supplied by producers, resulting in an economic equilibrium of price and quantity. The model incorporates other factors changing equilibrium as a shift of demand and/or supply.
   a. Deferred gratification
   b. Joint demand
   c. Rational addiction
   d. Supply and demand

6. _____ in economics and business is the result of an exchange and from that trade we assign a numerical monetary value to a good, service or asset. If Alice trades Bob 4 apples for an orange, the _____ of an orange is 4 apples. Inversely, the _____ of an apple is 1/4 oranges.
   a. Price
   b. Price book
   c. Premium pricing
   d. Price war

7. The _____ is the apparent contradiction that although water is on the whole more useful, in terms of survival, than diamonds, diamonds command a higher price in the market. The economist Adam Smith is often considered to be the classic presenter of this paradox. Nicolaus Copernicus, John Locke, John Law and others had previously tried to explain the disparity.
   a. St. Petersburg paradox
   b. 100-year flood
   c. 130-30 fund
   d. Paradox of value

8. In economics and finance, _____ is the change in total cost that arises when the quantity produced changes by one unit. It is the cost of producing one more unit of a good. Mathematically, the _____ function is expressed as the first derivative of the total cost (TC) function with respect to quantity (Q.)

Chapter 2. Fundamental Economic Concepts

a. Marginal cost
b. Quality costs
c. Khozraschyot
d. Variable cost

9. In economics the _____ of a good or service is the specific use to which an agent would put a given increase, or the specific use of the good or service that would be abandoned in response to a given decrease. The usefulness of the _____ thus corresponds to the marginal utility of the good or service.

On the assumption that an agent is economically rational, each increase would be put to the specific, feasible, previously unrealized use of greatest priority, and each decrease would result in abandonment of the use of lowest priority amongst the uses to which the good or service had been put.

a. 100-year flood
b. 1921 recession
c. 130-30 fund
d. Marginal use

10. In economics, the _____ of a good or of a service is the utility of the specific use to which an agent would put a given increase in that good or service, or of the specific use that would be abandoned in response to a given decrease. In other words, _____ is the utility of the marginal use -- which, on the assumption of economic rationality, would be the least urgent use of the good or service, from the best feasible combination of actions in which its use is included. Under the mainstream assumptions, the _____ of a good or service is the posited quantified change in utility obtained by increasing or by decreasing use of that good or service.

a. Marginal utility
b. 130-30 fund
c. 100-year flood
d. 1921 recession

11. In Marx's critique of political economy, any labor-product has a value and a _____, and if it is traded as a commodity in markets, it additionally has an exchange value, most often expressed as a money-price. Marx acknowledges that commodities being traded also have a general utility, implied by the fact that people want them, but he argues that this by itself tells us nothing about the specific character of the economy in which they are produced and sold.

The concepts of value, _____, utility, exchange value and price have a very long history in economic and philosophical thought, from Aristotle to Adam Smith, and their meanings evolved.

Chapter 2. Fundamental Economic Concepts 11

a. Accumulation by dispossession
b. Unreconstructed Marxism
c. Uneven and combined development
d. Use value

12.   In economics, _____ is a measure of the relative satisfaction from consumption of various goods and services. Given this measure, one may speak meaningfully of increasing or decreasing _____, and thereby explain economic behavior in terms of attempts to increase one's _____. For illustrative purposes, changes in _____ are sometimes expressed in units called utils.
   a. Expected utility hypothesis
   b. Ordinal utility
   c. Utility function
   d. Utility

13.   _____ is the a method of technical and economic research of the systems for purpose to optimize a parity between system's consumer functions or properties and expenses to achieve those functions or properties.

This methodology for continuous perfection of production, industrial technologies, organizational structures was developed by Juryj Sobolev in 1948 at the 'Perm telephone factory'

- 1948 Juryj Sobolev - the first success in application of a method analysis at the 'Perm telephone factory' .
- 1949 - the first application for the invention as result of use of the new method.

Today in economically developed countries practically each enterprise or the company use methodology of the kind of functional-cost analysis as a practice of the quality management, most full satisfying to principles of standards of series ISO 9000.

- Interest of consumer not in products itself, but the advantage which it will receive from its usage.
- The consumer aspires to reduce his expenses
- Functions needed by consumer can be executed in the various ways, and, hence, with various efficiency and expenses. Among possible alternatives of realization of functions exist such in which the parity of quality and the price is the optimal for the consumer.

The goal of _____ is achievement of the highest consumer satisfaction of production at simultaneous decrease in all kinds of industrial expenses Classical _____ has three English synonyms - Value Engineering, Value Management, Value Analysis.

a. Monopoly wage
b. Staple financing
c. Willingness to pay
d. Function cost analysis

14. In economics, the _____ can be defined as the graph depicting the relationship between the price of a certain commodity, and the amount of it that consumers are willing and able to purchase at that given price. It is a graphic representation of a demand schedule. The _____ for all consumers together follows from the _____ of every individual consumer: the individual demands at each price are added together.
   a. Wage curve
   b. Kuznets curve
   c. Demand curve
   d. Cost curve

15. In economics, a _____ is a table that lists the quantity of a good a person will buy it each different price See Demand curve.
   a. Demand schedule
   b. Federal Reserve districts
   c. Free contract
   d. Rational irrationality

16. In finance, the _____s between two currencies specifies how much one currency is worth in terms of the other. It is the value of a foreign natione;s currency in terms of the home natione;s currency. For example an _____ of 102 Japanese yen to the United States dollar means that JPY 102 is worth the same as USD 1.
   a. ACEA agreement
   b. ACCRA Cost of Living Index
   c. Interbank market
   d. Exchange rate

17. A _____ is an object whose consumption increases the utility of the consumer, for which the quantity demanded exceeds the quantity supplied at zero price. _____s are usually modeled as having diminishing marginal utility. The first individual purchase has high utility; the second has less.
   a. Composite good
   b. Merit good
   c. Good
   d. Pie method

Chapter 2. Fundamental Economic Concepts

18. _____ is a type of trade policy that allows traders to act and transact without interference from government. Thus, the policy permits trading partners mutual gains from trade, with goods and services produced according to the theory of comparative advantage.

Under a _____ policy, prices are a reflection of true supply and demand, and are the sole determinant of resource allocation.

   a. 100-year flood
   b. 1921 recession
   c. 130-30 fund
   d. Free Trade

19. The _____ is a trilateral trade bloc in North America created by the governments of the United States, Canada, and Mexico. The agreement creating the trade bloc came into force on January 1, 1994. It superseded the Canada-United States Free Trade Agreement between the U.S. and Canada.
   a. Federal Reserve Bank Notes
   b. Case-Shiller Home Price Indices
   c. Demand-side technologies
   d. North American Free Trade Agreement

20. _____ is the planning process used to determine whether a firm's long term investments such as new machinery, replacement machinery, new plants, new products, and research development projects are worth pursuing. It is budget for major capital, or investment, expenditures.

Many formal methods are used in _____, including the techniques such as

- Net present value
- Profitability index
- Internal rate of return
- Modified Internal Rate of Return
- Equivalent annuity

These methods use the incremental cash flows from each potential investment, or project. Techniques based on accounting earnings and accounting rules are sometimes used - though economists consider this to be improper - such as the accounting rate of return, and 'return on investment.' Simplified and hybrid methods are used as well, such as payback period and discounted payback period.

a. Participating preferred stock
b. Preferred stock
c. Voting interest
d. Capital budgeting

21. _____ or net present worth (NPW) is defined as the total present value (PV) of a time series of cash flows. It is a standard method for using the time value of money to appraise long-term projects. Used for capital budgeting, and widely throughout economics, it measures the excess or shortfall of cash flows, in present value terms, once financing charges are met.
   a. Maturity
   b. Refinancing risk
   c. Net present value
   d. Future value

22. _____ is the value on a given date of a future payment or series of future payments, discounted to reflect the time value of money and other factors such as investment risk. _____ calculations are widely used in business and economics to provide a means to compare cash flows at different times on a meaningful 'like to like' basis.

Money value fluctuates over time: $100 today are not worth $100 in five years.

   a. Present value of costs
   b. Tax shield
   c. Present value
   d. Future value

23. _____ refers to the movement of cash into or out of a business or financial product. It is usually measured during a specified, finite period of time. Measurement of _____ can be used

   - to determine a project's rate of return or value. The time of _____ s into and out of projects are used as inputs in financial models such as internal rate of return, and net present value.
   - to determine problems with a business's liquidity. Being profitable does not necessarily mean being liquid. A company can fail because of a shortage of cash, even while profitable.
   - as an alternate measure of a business's profits when it is believed that accrual accounting concepts do not represent economic realities. For example, a company may be notionally profitable but generating little operational cash (as may be the case for a company that barters its products rather than selling for cash.) In such a case, the company may be deriving additional operating cash by issuing shares evaluating default risk, re-investment requirements, etc.

   _____ is a generic term used differently depending on the context. It may be defined by users for their own purposes.

a. Strip financing
b. Second lien loan
c. Restricted stock
d. Cash flow

24. _____ is a way of expressing knowledge or belief that an event will occur or has occurred. In mathematics the concept has been given an exact meaning in _____ theory, that is used extensively in such areas of study as mathematics, statistics, finance, gambling, science, and philosophy to draw conclusions about the likelihood of potential events and the underlying mechanics of complex systems.

The word _____ does not have a consistent direct definition.

a. 100-year flood
b. Probability
c. 130-30 fund
d. 1921 recession

25. In probability theory and statistics, a _____ identifies either the probability of each value of an unidentified random variable (when the variable is discrete), or the probability of the value falling within a particular interval (when the variable is continuous.) The _____ describes the range of possible values that a random variable can attain and the probability that the value of the random variable is within any (measurable) subset of that range. The Normal distribution, often called the 'bell curve'

When the random variable takes values in the set of real numbers, the _____ is completely described by the cumulative distribution function, whose value at each real x is the probability that the random variable is smaller than or equal to x.

a. 130-30 fund
b. 100-year flood
c. 1921 recession
d. Probability distribution

26. In probability theory and statistics, _____ is a measure of the variability or dispersion of a population, a data set, or a probability distribution. A low _____ indicates that the data points tend to be very close to the same value (the mean), while high _____ indicates that the data are 'spread out' over a large range of values.

For example, the average height for adult men in the United States is about 70 inches, with a _____ of around 3 inches.

Chapter 2. Fundamental Economic Concepts

a. 130-30 fund
b. Standard deviation
c. 100-year flood
d. 1921 recession

27. In economics, _____ is a rise in the general level of prices of goods and services in an economy over a period of time. When the general price level rises, each unit of currency buys fewer goods and services; consequently, _____ is also a decline in the real value of money--a loss of purchasing power in the medium of exchange which is also the monetary unit of account in the economy. A chief measure of general price-level _____ is the general _____ rate, which is the percentage change in a general price index (normally the Consumer Price Index) over time.

a. Energy economics
b. Economic
c. Opportunity cost
d. Inflation

28. _____ was a U.S. hedge fund which used trading strategies such as fixed income arbitrage, statistical arbitrage, and pairs trading, combined with high leverage. It failed spectacularly in the late 1990s, leading to a massive bailout by other major banks and investment houses, which was supervised by the Federal Reserve.

LTCM was founded in 1994 by John Meriwether, the former vice-chairman and head of bond trading at Salomon Brothers.

a. Collectivization of agriculture in Romania
b. General purpose technologies
c. Consumer protection
d. Long-term capital management

29. In mathematics, a _____ is a constant multiplicative factor of a certain object. For example, in the expression $9x^2$, the _____ of x^2 is 9.

The object can be such things as a variable, a vector, a function, etc.

a. 130-30 fund
b. Coefficient
c. 1921 recession
d. 100-year flood

Chapter 2. Fundamental Economic Concepts

30. A _____ is the minimum difference a person requires to be willing to take an uncertain bet, between the expected value of the bet and the certain value that he is indifferent to.

The certainty equivalent is the guaranteed payoff at which a person is 'indifferent' between accepting the guaranteed payoff and a higher but uncertain payoff. (It is the amount of the higher payout minus the _____.)

   a. Linear model
   b. Ruin theory
   c. Workers compensation
   d. Risk premium

31. In finance, a _____ is a debt security, in which the authorized issuer owes the holders a debt and, depending on the terms of the _____, is obliged to pay interest (the coupon) and/or to repay the principal at a later date, termed maturity. A _____ is a formal contract to repay borrowed money with interest at fixed intervals.

Thus a _____ is like a loan: the issuer is the borrower (debtor), the holder is the lender (creditor), and the coupon is the interest.

   a. Zero-coupon
   b. Prize Bond
   c. Callable
   d. Bond

32. A _____ is a situation that involves losing one quality or aspect of something in return for gaining another quality or aspect. It implies a decision to be made with full comprehension of both the upside and downside of a particular choice.

In economics the term is expressed as opportunity cost, referring the most preferred alternative given up.

   a. Friedman-Savage utility function
   b. Whitemail
   c. Nonmarket
   d. Trade-off

33. _____s are financial contracts whose values are derived from the value of something else (known as the underlying.) The underlying value on which a _____ is based can be an asset (e.g., commodities, equities (stocks), residential mortgages, commercial real estate, loans, bonds), an index (e.g., interest rates, exchange rates, stock market indices, consumer price index (CPI) -- see inflation _____s), weather conditions bonds or other forms of credit.

a. 130-30 fund
b. Second derivative
c. 100-year flood
d. Derivative

Chapter 2. Fundamental Economic Concepts

34. A _____ is:

- Rewrite _____, in generative grammar and computer science
- Standardization, a formal and widely-accepted statement, fact, definition, or qualification
- Operation, a determinate _____ for performing a mathematical operation and obtaining a certain result (Mathematics, Logic)
    - Unary operation
    - Binary operation
- _____ of inference, a function from sets of formulae to formulae (Mathematics, Logic)
- _____ of thumb, principle with broad application that is not intended to be strictly accurate or reliable for every situation. Also often simply referred to as a _____
- Moral, an atomic element of a moral code for guiding choices in human behavior
- Heuristic, a quantized '_____' which shows a tendency or probability for successful function
- A regulation, as in sports
- A Production _____, as in computer science
- Procedural law, a _____ set governing the application of laws to cases
    - A law, which may informally be called a '_____'
    - A court ruling, a decision by a court
- In the U.S. Government, a regulation mandated by Congress, but written or expanded upon by the Executive Branch.
- Norm (sociology), an informal but widely accepted _____, concept, truth, definition, or qualification (social norms, legal norms, coding norms)
- Norm (philosophy), a kind of sentence or a reason to act, feel or believe
- 'Rulership' is the concept of governance by a government:
    - Military _____, governance by a military body
    - Monastic _____, a collection of precepts that guides the life of monks or nuns in a religious order where the superior holds the place of Christ
- Slide _____

- '_____,' a song by Ayumi Hamasaki
- '_____,' a song by rapper Nas
- '_____s,' an album by the band The Whitest Boy Alive
- _____s: Pyaar Ka Superhit Formula, a 2003 Bollywood film
- ruler, an instrument for measuring lengths
- _____, a component of an astrolabe, circumferator or similar instrument
- The _____s, a bestselling self-help book
- _____ Project (Run Up-to-date Linux Everywhere), a project that aims to use up-to-date Linux software on old PCs
- _____ engine, a software system that helps managing business _____s
- Ja _____, a hip hop artist
    - R.U.L.E., a 2005 greatest hits album by rapper Ja _____
- '_____s,' a KMFDM song

a. Rule
b. Procter ' Gamble
c. Technocracy
d. Demand

35. Let f be a differentiable function, and let f'(x) be its derivative. The derivative of f'(x) (if it has one) is written f''(x) and is called the _____ of f. Similarly, the derivative of a _____, if it exists, is written f'''(x) and is called the third derivative of f.
    a. 100-year flood
    b. 130-30 fund
    c. Weighted
    d. Second derivative

36. In economics, _____ is the process by which a firm determines the price and output level that returns the greatest profit. There are several approaches to this problem. The total revenue--total cost method relies on the fact that profit equals revenue minus cost, and the marginal revenue--marginal cost method is based on the fact that total profit in a perfectly competitive market reaches its maximum point where marginal revenue equals marginal cost.
    a. Profit margin
    b. Profit maximization
    c. 100-year flood
    d. Normal profit

37. In mathematics, a _____ of a function of several variables is its derivative with respect to one of those variables with the others held constant (as opposed to the total derivative, in which all variables are allowed to vary.) _____s are useful in vector calculus and differential geometry.

The _____ of a function f with respect to the variable x is written as f'_x, $\partial_x f$, or $\partial f/\partial x$.

    a. Partial derivative
    b. 100-year flood
    c. 1921 recession
    d. 130-30 fund

Chapter 3. Demand Analysis

1. Economics:

    - _____, the desire to own something and the ability to pay for it
    - _____ curve, a graphic representation of a _____ schedule
    - _____ deposit, the money in checking accounts
    - _____ pull theory, the theory that inflation occurs when _____ for goods and services exceeds existing supplies
    - _____ schedule, a table that lists the quantity of a good a person will buy it each different price
    - _____ side economics, the school of economics at believes government spending and tax cuts open economy by raising _____

    a. Production
    b. Variability
    c. Demand
    d. McKesson ' Robbins scandal

2. In economics, a _____ is a table that lists the quantity of a good a person will buy it each different price See Demand curve.
    a. Demand schedule
    b. Free contract
    c. Federal Reserve districts
    d. Rational irrationality

3. In economics, the _____ is the change in consumption resulting from a change in real income.

Another important item that can change is the money income of the consumer. The _____ is the phenomenon observed through changes in purchasing power.

    a. Export subsidy
    b. Inflation hedge
    c. Equilibrium wage
    d. Income effect

4. In economics, _____ is a measure of the relative satisfaction from consumption of various goods and services. Given this measure, one may speak meaningfully of increasing or decreasing _____, and thereby explain economic behavior in terms of attempts to increase one's _____. For illustrative purposes, changes in _____ are sometimes expressed in units called utils.

Chapter 3. Demand Analysis

   a. Utility function
   b. Utility
   c. Ordinal utility
   d. Expected utility hypothesis

5. In economics, a _____ or a hard good is a good which does not quickly wear out it yields services or utility over time rather than being completely used up when used once. Most goods are therefore _____s to a certain degree. These are goods that can last for a relatively long time, such as refrigerators, cars, and DVD players.
   a. Search good
   b. Luxury good
   c. Superior goods
   d. Durable good

6. A _____ is an object whose consumption increases the utility of the consumer, for which the quantity demanded exceeds the quantity supplied at zero price. _____s are usually modeled as having diminishing marginal utility. The first individual purchase has high utility; the second has less.
   a. Composite good
   b. Merit good
   c. Pie method
   d. Good

7. _____ in economics and business is the result of an exchange and from that trade we assign a numerical monetary value to a good, service or asset. If Alice trades Bob 4 apples for an orange, the _____ of an orange is 4 apples. Inversely, the _____ of an apple is 1/4 oranges.
   a. Price war
   b. Premium pricing
   c. Price
   d. Price book

8. _____ is defined as the measure of responsiveness in the quantity demanded for a commodity as a result of change in price of the same commodity. It is a measure of how consumers react to a change in price. In other words, it is percentage change in quantity demanded as per the percentage change in price of the same commodity.
   a. 100-year flood
   b. 1921 recession
   c. Price elasticity of demand
   d. 130-30 fund

Chapter 3. Demand Analysis

9. In economics, _____ is the ratio of the percent change in one variable to the percent change in another variable. It is a tool for measuring the responsiveness of a function to changes in parameters in a relative way. Commonly analyzed are _____ of substitution, price and wealth.
   a. ACCRA Cost of Living Index
   b. Elasticity of demand
   c. ACEA agreement
   d. Elasticity

10. Price _____ is defined as the measure of responsiveness in the quantity demanded for a commodity as a result of change in price of the same commodity. It is a measure of how consumers react to a change in price. In other words, it is percentage change in quantity demanded by the percentage change in price of the same commodity.
    a. Elasticity
    b. ACCRA Cost of Living Index
    c. ACEA agreement
    d. Elasticity of demand

11. CÄ"terÄ«s paribus is a Latin phrase, literally translated as 'with other things the same.' It is commonly rendered in English as 'all other things being equal.' A prediction, or a statement about causal or logical connections between two states of affairs, is qualified by _____ in order to acknowledge, and to rule out, the possibility of other factors which could override the relationship between the antecedent and the consequent.

    A _____ assumption is often fundamental to the predictive purpose of scientific inquiry. In order to formulate scientific laws, it is usually necessary to rule out factors which interfere with examining a specific causal relationship.

    a. Friedman-Savage utility function
    b. Capital outflow
    c. Dematerialization
    d. Ceteris paribus

12. In microeconomics, _____ is the extra revenue that an additional unit of product will bring. It is the additional income from selling one more unit of a good; sometimes equal to price. It can also be described as the change in total revenue/change in number of units sold.
    a. Long term
    b. Market demand schedule
    c. Reservation price
    d. Marginal revenue

13. _____ is a broad label that refers to any individuals or households that use goods and services generated within the economy. The concept of a _____ is used in different contexts, so that the usage and significance of the term may vary.

Typically when business people and economists talk of _____s they are talking about person as _____, an aggregated commodity item with little individuality other than that expressed in the buy/not-buy decision.

   a. 1921 recession
   b. 130-30 fund
   c. Consumer
   d. 100-year flood

14. _____ is a type of trade policy that allows traders to act and transact without interference from government. Thus, the policy permits trading partners mutual gains from trade, with goods and services produced according to the theory of comparative advantage.

Under a _____ policy, prices are a reflection of true supply and demand, and are the sole determinant of resource allocation.

   a. 130-30 fund
   b. 1921 recession
   c. 100-year flood
   d. Free trade

15. In economics, the _____ of demand measures the responsiveness of the demand of a good to the change in the income of the people demanding the good. It is calculated as the ratio of the percent change in demand to the percent change in income. For example, if, in response to a 10% increase in income, the demand of a good increased by 20%, the _____ of demand would be 20%/10% = 2.
   a. ACCRA Cost of Living Index
   b. AD-IA Model
   c. ACEA agreement
   d. Income elasticity

16. Competition law, known in the United States as _____ law, has three main elements:

- prohibiting agreements or practices that restrict free trading and competition between business entities. This includes in particular the repression of cartels.
- banning abusive behaviour by a firm dominating a market, or anti-competitive practices that tend to lead to such a dominant position. Practices controlled in this way may include predatory pricing, tying, price gouging, refusal to deal, and many others.
- supervising the mergers and acquisitions of large corporations, including some joint ventures. Transactions that are considered to threaten the competitive process can be prohibited altogether, or approved subject to 'remedies' such as an obligation to divest part of the merged business or to offer licences or access to facilities to enable other businesses to continue competing.

The substance and practice of competition law varies from jurisdiction to jurisdiction. Protecting the interests of consumers (consumer welfare) and ensuring that entrepreneurs have an opportunity to compete in the market economy are often treated as important objectives. Competition law is closely connected with law on deregulation of access to markets, state aids and subsidies, the privatisation of state owned assets and the establishment of independent sector regulators. In recent decades, competition law has been viewed as a way to provide better public services.

a. Intellectual property law
b. United Kingdom competition law
c. Anti-Inflation Act
d. Antitrust

17. The _____ is an independent agency of the United States government, established in 1914 by the _____ Act. Its principal mission is the promotion of 'consumer protection' and the elimination and prevention of what regulators perceive to be harmfully 'anti-competitive' business practices, such as coercive monopoly.

The _____ Act was one of President Wilson's major acts against trusts.

a. 100-year flood
b. 1921 recession
c. Federal Trade Commission
d. 130-30 fund

Chapter 4. Estimating Demand

1. _____ is a broad label that refers to any individuals or households that use goods and services generated within the economy. The concept of a _____ is used in different contexts, so that the usage and significance of the term may vary.

Typically when business people and economists talk of _____s they are talking about person as _____, an aggregated commodity item with little individuality other than that expressed in the buy/not-buy decision.

   a. 130-30 fund
   b. 1921 recession
   c. 100-year flood
   d. Consumer

2. Economics:

   - _____,the desire to own something and the ability to pay for it
   - _____ curve,a graphic representation of a _____ schedule
   - _____ deposit, the money in checking accounts
   - _____ pull theory,the theory that inflation occurs when _____ for goods and services exceeds existing supplies
   - _____ schedule,a table that lists the quantity of a good a person will buy it each different price
   - _____ side economics,the school of economics at believes government spending and tax cuts open economy by raising _____

   a. Variability
   b. Production
   c. McKesson ' Robbins scandal
   d. Demand

3. _____s are expenses that change in proportion to the activity of a business. In other words, _____ is the sum of marginal costs. It can also be considered normal costs.
   a. Variable cost
   b. Cost-Volume-Profit Analysis
   c. Cost allocation
   d. Quality costs

4. In statistics, given a (random) sample $(Y_i, X_{i1}, \ldots, X_{ip}), i = 1, \ldots, n$ the most general form of _____ is formulated as

$$Y_i = \beta_0 + \beta_1 \phi_1(X_{i1}) + \ldots + \beta_p \phi_p(X_{ip}) + \varepsilon_i \qquad i = 1, \ldots, n$$

where $\phi_1, \ldots, \phi_p$ may be nonlinear functions.

In matrix notation this model can be written as

$$Y = X\beta + \varepsilon$$

where Y is an n × 1 column vector, X is an n × (p + 1) matrix, β is a (p + 1) × 1 vector of (unobservable) parameters, and ε is an n × 1 vector of errors, which are uncorrelated random variables each with expected value 0 and variance σ^2. Note that depending on the context the sample can be seen as fixed (observable), or random.

a. Ruin theory
b. Workers compensation
c. Linear model
d. RiskMetrics

5. In statistics, _____ is used for two things;

- to construct a simple formula that will predict a value or values for a variable given the value of another variable.
- to test whether and how a given variable is related to another variable or variables.

Note: correlation does not imply causation.

_____ is a form of regression analysis in which the relationship between one or more independent variables and another variable, called the dependent variable, is modelled by a least squares function, called a _____ equation. This function is a linear combination of one or more model parameters, called regression coefficients. A _____ equation with one independent variable represents a straight line when the predicted value (i.e. the dependant variable from the regression equation) is plotted against the independent variable: this is called a simple _____.

a. Nonlinear regression
b. Polynomial regression
c. Linear regression
d. Mathematical statistics

6. A _____ is a linear regression in which there is only one covariate (predictor variable.)

_____ is used to evaluate the linear relationship between two variables. One example could be the relationship between muscle strength and lean body mass.

  a. Multivariate adaptive regression splines
  b. Stepwise regression
  c. Trend analysis
  d. Simple linear regression

7. In mathematics, a _____ is a constant multiplicative factor of a certain object. For example, in the expression $9x^2$, the _____ of x^2 is 9.

The object can be such things as a variable, a vector, a function, etc.

  a. Coefficient
  b. 130-30 fund
  c. 1921 recession
  d. 100-year flood

8. In statistics, _____ indicates the strength and direction of a linear relationship between two random variables. That is in contrast with the usage of the term in colloquial speech, which denotes any relationship, not necessarily linear. In general statistical usage, _____ or co-relation refers to the departure of two random variables from independence.
  a. 100-year flood
  b. 1921 recession
  c. 130-30 fund
  d. Correlation

9. In statistics, _____ has two related meanings:

   - the arithmetic _____
   - the expected value of a random variable, which is also called the population _____.

It is sometimes stated that the '_____' _____s average. This is incorrect if '_____' is taken in the specific sense of 'arithmetic _____' as there are different types of averages: the _____, median, and mode. Other simple statistical analyses use measures of spread, such as range, interquartile range, or standard deviation. For a real-valued random variable X, the _____ is the expectation of X. Note that not every probability distribution has a defined _____ (or variance); see the Cauchy distribution for an example.

a. Mean
b. 100-year flood
c. 130-30 fund
d. 1921 recession

10. In statistics, the _____, R^2 is used in the context of statistical models whose main purpose is the prediction of future outcomes on the basis of other related information. It is the proportion of variability in a data set that is accounted for by the statistical model. It provides a measure of how well future outcomes are likely to be predicted by the model.
  a. Partial leverage
  b. Feasible generalized least squares
  c. DFFITS
  d. Coefficient of determination

11. _____ is the cross-correlation of a signal with itself. It is a mathematical tool for finding repeating patterns, such as the presence of a periodic signal which has been buried under noise, or identifying the missing fundamental frequency in a signal implied by its harmonic frequencies. It is used frequently in signal processing for analyzing functions or series of values, such as time domain signals.
  a. ACEA agreement
  b. AD-IA Model
  c. Autocorrelation
  d. ACCRA Cost of Living Index

12. _____ is a statistical phenomenon in which two or more predictor variables in a multiple regression model are highly correlated. In this situation the coefficient estimates may change erratically in response to small changes in the model or the data. _____ does not reduce the predictive power or reliability of the model as a whole; it only affects calculations regarding individual predictors.
  a. Generalized additive model
  b. Total sum of squares
  c. Quantile regression
  d. Multicollinearity

13. In mathematics, a _____ system is a system which is not linear, that is, a system which does not satisfy the superposition principle, or whose output is not proportional to its input. Less technically, a _____ system is any problem where the variable(s) to be solved for cannot be written as a linear combination of independent components. A nonhomogeneous system, which is linear apart from the presence of a function of the independent variables, is _____ according to a strict definition, but such systems are usually studied alongside linear systems, because they can be transformed to a linear system of multiple variables.

a. Nonlinear
b. 100-year flood
c. 130-30 fund
d. Nonlinear system

14. In statistics, _____ is a form of regression analysis in which observational data are modeled by a function which is a nonlinear combination of the model parameters and depends on one or more independent variables. The data are fitted by a method of successive approximations.

The data consist of error-free independent variables (explanatory variable), x, and their associated observed dependent variables (response variable), y.

a. Mathematical statistics
b. Confidence interval
c. Statistically significant
d. Nonlinear regression

Chapter 5. Business and Economic Forecasting

1. _____s is the social science that studies the production, distribution, and consumption of goods and services. The term _____s comes from the Ancient Greek οἰκονομία from οἶκος (oikos, 'house') + νόμος (nomos, 'custom' or 'law'), hence 'rules of the house(hold)'. Current _____ models developed out of the broader field of political economy in the late 19th century, owing to a desire to use an empirical approach more akin to the physical sciences.
   a. Inflation
   b. Economic
   c. Opportunity cost
   d. Energy economics

2. _____ is the process of making predictions about the economy as a whole or in part.

Relevant models include

- Economic base analysis
- Shift-share analysis
- Input-output model
- Grinold and Kroner Model

   a. Australian Financial Services Licence
   b. Overproduction
   c. Investment goods
   d. Economic forecasting

3. _____ is the process of estimation in unknown situations. Prediction is a similar, but more general term. Both can refer to estimation of time series, cross-sectional or longitudinal data.
   a. 130-30 fund
   b. Forecasting
   c. 100-year flood
   d. 1921 recession

4. _____ or cross section (of a study population) in statistics and econometrics is a type of one-dimensional data set. _____ refers to data collected by observing many subjects (such as individuals, firms or countries/regions) at the same point of time, or without regard to differences in time. Analysis of _____ usually consists of comparing the differences among the subjects.
   a. Cross-sectional data
   b. 1921 recession
   c. 100-year flood
   d. 130-30 fund

5. The term '_____' refers to the concept of collecting information and attempting to spot a pattern in the information. In some fields of study, the term '_____' has more formally-defined meanings.

In project management _____ is a mathematical technique that uses historical results to predict future outcome.

   a. Trend analysis
   b. Coefficient of determination
   c. Quantile regression
   d. Probit model

6. In economics, _____ is a rise in the general level of prices of goods and services in an economy over a period of time. When the general price level rises, each unit of currency buys fewer goods and services; consequently, _____ is also a decline in the real value of money--a loss of purchasing power in the medium of exchange which is also the monetary unit of account in the economy. A chief measure of general price-level _____ is the general _____ rate, which is the percentage change in a general price index (normally the Consumer Price Index) over time.
   a. Opportunity cost
   b. Economic
   c. Energy economics
   d. Inflation

7. In statistics and image processing, to smooth a data set is to create an approximating function that attempts to capture important patterns in the data, while leaving out noise or other fine-scale structures/rapid phenomena. Many different algorithms are used in _____. One of the most common algorithms is the 'moving average', often used to try to capture important trends in repeated statistical surveys.
   a. Partial residual plot
   b. X-bar chart
   c. Partial regression plot
   d. Smoothing

8. In statistics, a _____ is used to analyze a set of data points by creating a series of averages of different subsets of the full data set. So a _____ is not a single number, but it is a set of numbers, each of which is the average of the corresponding subset of a larger set of data points. A simple example is if you had a data set with 100 data points, the first value of the _____ might be the arithmetic mean of data points 1 through 25.
   a. Failure rate
   b. Time series
   c. Moving average
   d. Type I error

9. In statistics, _____ is a technique that can be applied to time series data, either to produce smoothed data for presentation, or to make forecasts. The time series data themselves are a sequence of observations. The observed phenomenon may be an essentially random process, or it may be an orderly, but noisy, process.
   a. Autoregressive conditional heteroskedasticity
   b. Exponential smoothing
   c. Innovations vector
   d. Unit root

10. _____ in economics and business is the result of an exchange and from that trade we assign a numerical monetary value to a good, service or asset. If Alice trades Bob 4 apples for an orange, the _____ of an orange is 4 apples. Inversely, the _____ of an apple is 1/4 oranges.
   a. Premium pricing
   b. Price book
   c. Price war
   d. Price

11. In economics, _____ are key economic variables that economists used to predict a new phase of the business cycle. A leading indicator is one that changes before the economy does; a lagging indicator is one that changes after the economy has changed. Examples of _____ include stock prices, which often improve or worsen before a similar change in the economy.
   a. Macroeconomics
   b. Medium of exchange
   c. Gross domestic product
   d. Leading indicators

12. _____s is concerned with the tasks of developing and applying quantitative or statistical methods to the study and elucidation of economic principles. _____s combines economic theory with statistics to analyze and test economic relationships. Theoretical _____s considers questions about the statistical properties of estimators and tests, while applied _____s is concerned with the application of _____ methods to assess economic theories.
   a. Evolutionary economics
   b. Experimental economics
   c. Econometric
   d. Economic

13. _____s are statistical models used in econometrics. An _____ specifies the statistical relationship that is believed to hold between the various economic quantities pertaining a particular economic phenomena under study. An _____ can be derived from a deterministic economic model by allowing for uncertainty or from an economic model which itself is stochastic.

a. Event study
b. Economic statistics
c. ACCRA Cost of Living Index
d. Econometric model

14. The _____ is the largest national economy in the world. Its gross domestic product (GDP) was estimated as $14.2 trillion in 2008. The U.S. economy maintains a high level of output per person (GDP per capita, $46,800 in 2008, ranked at around number ten in the world.)
a. Economy of the United States
b. ACEA agreement
c. ACCRA Cost of Living Index
d. AD-IA Model

15. _____ means random.

A _____ process is one whose behavior is non-deterministic in that a system's subsequent state is determined both by the process's predictable actions and by a random element. _____ crafts are complex systems whose practitioners, even if complete experts, acknowledge that outcomes result from both known and unknown causes.

a. Theory
b. 130-30 fund
c. 100-year flood
d. Stochastic

16. In statistics, signal processing, and many other fields, a _____ is a sequence of data points, measured typically at successive times, spaced at (often uniform) time intervals. _____ analysis comprises methods that attempt to understand such _____, often either to understand the underlying context of the data points (Where did they come from? What generated them?), or to make forecasts (predictions.) _____ forecasting is the use of a model to forecast future events based on known past events: to forecast future data points before they are measured.
a. Nonlinear regression
b. Time series
c. First-hitting-time models
d. Heteroskedastic

17. _____ was a U.S. hedge fund which used trading strategies such as fixed income arbitrage, statistical arbitrage, and pairs trading, combined with high leverage. It failed spectacularly in the late 1990s, leading to a massive bailout by other major banks and investment houses, which was supervised by the Federal Reserve.

LTCM was founded in 1994 by John Meriwether, the former vice-chairman and head of bond trading at Salomon Brothers.

   a. General purpose technologies
   b. Consumer protection
   c. Long-term capital management
   d. Collectivization of agriculture in Romania

Chapter 6. Managing Exports

1. In economics, an _____ is any good or commodity, transported from one country to another country in a legitimate fashion, typically for use in trade. _____ goods or services are provided to foreign consumers by domestic producers. _____ is an important part of international trade.

   a. ACEA agreement
   b. Export
   c. ACCRA Cost of Living Index
   d. AD-IA Model

2. _____ is one of the four Ps of the marketing mix. The other three aspects are product, promotion, and place. It is also a key variable in microeconomic price allocation theory.

   a. Point of total assumption
   b. Premium pricing
   c. Guaranteed Maximum Price
   d. Pricing

3. In finance, the _____s between two currencies specifies how much one currency is worth in terms of the other. It is the value of a foreign natione;s currency in terms of the home natione;s currency. For example an _____ of 102 Japanese yen to the United States dollar means that JPY 102 is worth the same as USD 1.

   a. ACCRA Cost of Living Index
   b. Interbank market
   c. ACEA agreement
   d. Exchange rate

4. The _____ is where currency trading takes place. It is where banks and other official institutions facilitate the buying and selling of foreign currencies. FX transactions typically involve one party purchasing a quantity of one currency in exchange for paying a quantity of another.

   a. Foreign exchange market
   b. Covered interest arbitrage
   c. Currency swap
   d. Floating currency

5. _____ is a financial term which measures the proportion of money invested in the same industry sector. For example, a stock portfolio with a total worth of $500,000, with $100,000 in semiconductor industry stocks, would have a 20% exposure in 'chip' stocks.

Chapter 6. Managing Exports 37

   a. Random walk hypothesis
   b. Put-call parity
   c. Martingale pricing
   d. Market exposure

6. _____ describes a deliberate attempt to interfere with the free and fair operation of the market and create artificial, false or misleading appearances with respect to the price of a security, commodity or currency. _____ is prohibited under Section 9(a)(2) of the Securities Exchange Act of 1934, and in Australia under Section s 1041A of the Corporations Act 2001. The Act defines _____ as transactions which create an artificial price or maintain an artificial price for a tradable security.
   a. Legal monopoly
   b. Market manipulation
   c. Managerial economics
   d. Net domestic product

7. Currency risk is a form of risk that arises from the change in price of one currency against another. Whenever investors or companies have assets or business operations across national borders, they face currency risk if their positions are not hedged.

   - _____ is the risk that exchange rates will change unfavourably over time. It can be hedged against using forward currency contracts;
   - Translation risk is an accounting risk, proportional to the amount of assets held in foreign currencies. Changes in the exchange rate over time will render a report inaccurate, and so assets are usually balanced by borrowings in that currency.

The exchange risk associated with a foreign denominated instrument is a key element in foreign investment. This risk flows from differential monetary policy and growth in real productivity, which results in differential inflation rates.

   a. Taleb distribution
   b. Currency risk
   c. Risk neutral
   d. Transaction risk

8. _____ is subcontracting a process, such as product design or manufacturing, to a third-party company. The decision to outsource is often made in the interest of lowering cost or making better use of time and energy costs, redirecting or conserving energy directed at the competencies of a particular business, or to make more efficient use of land, labor, capital, (information) technology and resources. _____ became part of the business lexicon during the 1980s.

Chapter 6. Managing Exports

a. Additional Funds Needed
b. Electronic business
c. Averch-Johnson effect
d. Outsourcing

9. In economics, an _____ is any good (e.g. a commodity) or service brought into one country from another country in a legitimate fashion, typically for use in trade. It is a good that is brought in from another country for sale. _____ goods or services are provided to domestic consumers by foreign producers. An _____ in the receiving country is an export to the sending country.

a. Economic integration
b. Import quota
c. Incoterms
d. Import

10. _____ is money accepted for exchange of goods in an economy. The prevalence of one money over another arises, usually, when a government designates through decrees that the government shall accept only particular notes and coins in payment for taxes. Typically, money of _____ consists of stamped coins and minted paper bills.

a. Totnes pound
b. Currency
c. Security thread
d. Local currency

11. Economics:

- _____, the desire to own something and the ability to pay for it
- _____ curve, a graphic representation of a _____ schedule
- _____ deposit, the money in checking accounts
- _____ pull theory, the theory that inflation occurs when _____ for goods and services exceeds existing supplies
- _____ schedule, a table that lists the quantity of a good a person will buy it each different price
- _____ side economics, the school of economics at believes government spending and tax cuts open economy by raising _____

a. McKesson ' Robbins scandal
b. Variability
c. Demand
d. Production

Chapter 6. Managing Exports

12. _____ in economics and business is the result of an exchange and from that trade we assign a numerical monetary value to a good, service or asset. If Alice trades Bob 4 apples for an orange, the _____ of an orange is 4 apples. Inversely, the _____ of an apple is 1/4 oranges.
    a. Price war
    b. Premium pricing
    c. Price
    d. Price book

13. _____ is the demand for financial assets, such as securities, money or foreign currency that is not dictated by real transactions such as trade, or financing.

The need for cash to take advantage of investment opportunities that may arise.

In economic theory, specifically Keynesian economics, _____ is one of the determinants of demand for money (and credit), the others being transactions demand and precautionary demand.

    a. Multiplier effect
    b. Spending multiplier
    c. Keynesian Revolution
    d. Speculative demand

14. In economics and finance, _____ is the practice of taking advantage of a price differential between two or more markets: striking a combination of matching deals that capitalize upon the imbalance, the profit being the difference between the market prices. When used by academics, an _____ is a transaction that involves no negative cash flow at any probabilistic or temporal state and a positive cash flow in at least one state; in simple terms, a risk-free profit. A person who engages in _____ is called an arbitrageur--such as a bank or brokerage firm.
    a. Alternext
    b. Electronic trading
    c. Options Price Reporting Authority
    d. Arbitrage

15. In finance, _____ is a financial action that does not promise safety of the initial investment along with the return on the principal sum. _____ typically involves the lending of money or the purchase of assets, equity or debt but in a manner that has not been given thorough analysis or is deemed to have low margin of safety or a significant risk of the loss of the principal investment. The term, '_____,' which is formally defined as above in Graham and Dodd's 1934 text, Security Analysis, contrasts with the term 'investment,' which is a financial operation that, upon thorough analysis, promises safety of principal and a satisfactory return.

a. Municipal Bond Arbitrage
b. Global Financial Centres Index
c. Speculation
d. Hybrid market

16. _____ is the identification, assessment, and prioritization of risks followed by coordinated and economical application of resources to minimize, monitor, and control the probability and/or impact of unfortunate events.. Risks can come from uncertainty in financial markets, project failures, legal liabilities, credit risk, accidents, natural causes and disasters as well as deliberate attacks from an adversary. Several _____ standards have been developed including the Project Management Institute, the National Institute of Science ' Technology, actuarial societies, and ISO standards.
    a. Risk management
    b. Kanban
    c. Regression toward the mean
    d. Penny stock

17. In algebra, a _____ is a function depending on n that associates a scalar, det(A), to an n×n square matrix A. The fundamental geometric meaning of a _____ is a scale factor for measure when A is regarded as a linear transformation. _____s are important both in calculus, where they enter the substitution rule for several variables, and in multilinear algebra.

For a fixed nonnegative integer n, there is a unique _____ function for the n×n matrices over any commutative ring R. In particular, this function exists when R is the field of real or complex numbers.

   a. 100-year flood
   b. Determinant
   c. 1921 recession
   d. 130-30 fund

18. In economic models, the _____ time frame assumes no fixed factors of production. Firms can enter or leave the marketplace, and the cost (and availability) of land, labor, raw materials, and capital goods can be assumed to vary. In contrast, in the short-run time frame, certain factors are assumed to be fixed, because there is not sufficient time for them to change.
    a. Price/performance ratio
    b. Diseconomies of scale
    c. Productivity world
    d. Long-run

Chapter 6. Managing Exports

19. The term '_____' refers to the concept of collecting information and attempting to spot a pattern in the information. In some fields of study, the term '_____' has more formally-defined meanings.

In project management _____ is a mathematical technique that uses historical results to predict future outcome.

   a. Quantile regression
   b. Coefficient of determination
   c. Probit model
   d. Trend analysis

20. _____ is the a method of technical and economic research of the systems for purpose to optimize a parity between system's consumer functions or properties and expenses to achieve those functions or properties.

This methodology for continuous perfection of production, industrial technologies, organizational structures was developed by Juryj Sobolev in 1948 at the 'Perm telephone factory'

- 1948 Juryj Sobolev - the first success in application of a method analysis at the 'Perm telephone factory' .
- 1949 - the first application for the invention as result of use of the new method.

Today in economically developed countries practically each enterprise or the company use methodology of the kind of functional-cost analysis as a practice of the quality management, most full satisfying to principles of standards of series ISO 9000.

- Interest of consumer not in products itself, but the advantage which it will receive from its usage.
- The consumer aspires to reduce his expenses
- Functions needed by consumer can be executed in the various ways, and, hence, with various efficiency and expenses. Among possible alternatives of realization of functions exist such in which the parity of quality and the price is the optimal for the consumer.

The goal of _____ is achievement of the highest consumer satisfaction of production at simultaneous decrease in all kinds of industrial expenses Classical _____ has three English synonyms - Value Engineering, Value Management, Value Analysis.

   a. Monopoly wage
   b. Staple financing
   c. Willingness to pay
   d. Function cost analysis

Chapter 6. Managing Exports

21. _____ is a fee paid on borrowed assets. It is the price paid for the use of borrowed money, or, money earned by deposited funds. Assets that are sometimes lent with _____ include money, shares, consumer goods through hire purchase, major assets such as aircraft, and even entire factories in finance lease arrangements.

   a. Asset protection
   b. Internal debt
   c. Insolvency
   d. Interest

22. An _____ is the price a borrower pays for the use of money they do not own, for instance a small company might borrow from a bank to kick start their business, and the return a lender receives for deferring the use of funds, by lending it to the borrower. _____s are normally expressed as a percentage rate over the period of one year.

_____s targets are also a vital tool of monetary policy and are used to control variables like investment, inflation, and unemployment.

   a. Enterprise value
   b. ACCRA Cost of Living Index
   c. Arrow-Debreu model
   d. Interest rate

23. The '_____' is approximately the nominal interest rate minus the inflation rate Since the inflation rate over the course of a loan is not known initially, volatility in inflation represents a risk to both the lender and the borrower.

In economics and finance, an individual who lends money for repayment at a later point in time expects to be compensated for the time value of money, or not having the use of that money while it is lent.

   a. Cost-push inflation
   b. Real interest rate
   c. Core inflation
   d. Reflation

24. In economics, _____ is a rise in the general level of prices of goods and services in an economy over a period of time. When the general price level rises, each unit of currency buys fewer goods and services; consequently, _____ is also a decline in the real value of money--a loss of purchasing power in the medium of exchange which is also the monetary unit of account in the economy. A chief measure of general price-level _____ is the general _____ rate, which is the percentage change in a general price index (normally the Consumer Price Index) over time.

a. Energy economics
b. Inflation
c. Opportunity cost
d. Economic

25. _____ refers to a business or organization attempting to acquire goods or services to accomplish the goals of the enterprise. Though there are several organizations that attempt to set standards in the _____ process, processes can vary greatly between organizations. Typically the word '_____' is not used interchangeably with the word 'procurement', since procurement typically includes Expediting, Supplier Quality, and Traffic and Logistics (T'L) in addition to _____.
   a. Free port
   b. 100-year flood
   c. 130-30 fund
   d. Purchasing

26. _____ is the number of goods/services that can be purchased with a unit of currency. For example, if you had taken one dollar to a store in the 1950s, you would have been able to buy a greater number of items than you would today, indicating that you would have had a greater _____ in the 1950s. Currency can be either a commodity money, like gold or silver, or fiat currency like US dollars.
   a. Compliance cost
   b. Genuine progress indicator
   c. Human Poverty Index
   d. Purchasing power

27. The _____ theory uses the long-term equilibrium exchange rate of two currencies to equalize their purchasing power. Developed by Gustav Cassel in 1920, it is based on the law of one price: the theory states that, in ideally efficient markets, identical goods should have only one price.

This purchasing power SEM rate equalizes the purchasing power of different currencies in their home countries for a given basket of goods.

   a. Gross national product
   b. Measures of national income and output
   c. Bureau of Labor Statistics
   d. Purchasing power parity

Chapter 6. Managing Exports

28. A _____ is an entity formed between two or more parties to undertake economic activity together. The parties agree to create a new entity by both contributing equity, and they then share in the revenues, expenses, and control of the enterprise. The venture can be for one specific project only, or a continuing business relationship such as the Fuji Xerox _____.
   a. Business valuation
   b. Property right
   c. Nexus of contracts
   d. Joint venture

29. An _____ is a person who has possession of an enterprise and assumes significant accountability for the inherent risks and the outcome. It is an ambitious leader who combines land, labor, and capital to create and market new goods or services. The term is a loanword from French and was first defined by the Irish economist Richard Cantillon.
   a. ACCRA Cost of Living Index
   b. ACEA agreement
   c. Expansionary policies
   d. Entrepreneur

30. _____ is a type of trade policy that allows traders to act and transact without interference from government. Thus, the policy permits trading partners mutual gains from trade, with goods and services produced according to the theory of comparative advantage.

Under a _____ policy, prices are a reflection of true supply and demand, and are the sole determinant of resource allocation.

   a. 100-year flood
   b. 130-30 fund
   c. 1921 recession
   d. Free Trade

31. The _____ is a trilateral trade bloc in North America created by the governments of the United States, Canada, and Mexico. The agreement creating the trade bloc came into force on January 1, 1994. It superseded the Canada-United States Free Trade Agreement between the U.S. and Canada.
   a. Case-Shiller Home Price Indices
   b. North American Free Trade Agreement
   c. Federal Reserve Bank Notes
   d. Demand-side technologies

32. In economics, _____ refers to the ability of a person or a country to produce a particular good at a lower marginal cost and opportunity cost than another person or country. It is the ability to produce a product most efficiently given all the other products that could be produced. It can be contrasted with absolute advantage which refers to the ability of a person or a country to produce a particular good at a lower absolute cost than another.
   a. Gravity model of trade
   b. Comparative advantage
   c. Hot money
   d. Triffin dilemma

33. In economics, the _____ is the idea that a nation is better off when it produces goods and services for which it has a comparative advantage.
   a. Monopolistic competition
   b. Keynesian economics
   c. Recession
   d. Law of comparative advantage

34. In economics, _____ is the ratio of the percent change in one variable to the percent change in another variable. It is a tool for measuring the responsiveness of a function to changes in parameters in a relative way. Commonly analyzed are _____ of substitution, price and wealth.
   a. ACCRA Cost of Living Index
   b. Elasticity of demand
   c. ACEA agreement
   d. Elasticity

35. In economics, _____ refers to the ability of a party to produce a good or service using fewer real resources than another entity producing the same good or service..A party has an _____ when using the same input as another party, it can produce a greater output. Since _____ is determined by a simple comparison of labor productivities, it is possible for a a party to have no _____ in anything. It can be contrasted with the concept of comparative advantage which refers to the ability to produce a particular good at a lower opportunity cost.
   a. Index number
   b. Absolute advantage
   c. ACCRA Cost of Living Index
   d. International economics

36. In international economics and international trade, _____ or _____ is the relative prices of a country's export to import. '_____' are sometimes used as a proxy for the relative social welfare of a country, but this heuristic is technically questionable and should be used with extreme caution. An improvement in a nation's _____ is good for that country in the sense that it has to pay less for the products it import.

a. Kennedy Round
b. Commercial invoice
c. Common market
d. Terms of trade

37. A _____ is a duty imposed on goods when they are moved across a political boundary. They are usually associated with protectionism, the economic policy of restraining trade between nations. For political reasons, _____s are usually imposed on imported goods, although they may also be imposed on exported goods.
   a. 130-30 fund
   b. Tariff
   c. 100-year flood
   d. 1921 recession

38. The _____ is an economic and political union of 27 member states, located primarily in Europe. It was established by the Treaty of Maastricht on 1 November 1993, upon the foundations of the pre-existing European Economic Community. With a population of almost 500 million, the _____ generates an estimated 30% share (US$18.4 trillion in 2008) of the nominal gross world product.
   a. European Union
   b. ACCRA Cost of Living Index
   c. European Court of Justice
   d. ACEA agreement

39. _____ is a designated group of countries that have agreed to eliminate tariffs, quotas and preferences on most (if not all) goods and services traded between them. It can be considered the second stage of economic integration. Countries choose this kind of economic integration form if their economical structures are complementary.
   a. MERCOSUR
   b. Free trade area
   c. 100-year flood
   d. 130-30 fund

40. A _____ is the trade of a commodity through distribution channels which, while legal, are unofficial, unauthorized, or unintended by the original manufacturer. In contrast, a black market is the trade of goods and services that are illegal in themselves and/or distributed through illegal channels, such as the selling of stolen goods or illegal items such as heroin or unregistered handguns.

The two main types of _____ are imported manufactured goods that would normally be unavailable or more expensive in a certain country and unissued securities that are not yet traded in official markets.

a. Mutual recognition agreement
b. Certificate of origin
c. Merchant bank
d. Grey market

41. The balance of trade (or net exports, sometimes symbolized as NX) is the difference between the monetary value of exports and imports in an economy over a certain period of time. It is the relationship between a nation's imports and exports. A favorable balance of trade is known as a trade surplus and consists of exporting more than is imported; an unfavorable balance of trade is known as a _____ or, informally, a trade gap.
    a. Trade deficit
    b. Computational economic
    c. Complementary asset
    d. Demographics of India

42. In Marxian economics, _____ originally referred to the means of production. Individuals, organizations and governments use _____ in the production of other goods or commodities. _____ include factories, machinery, tools, equipment, and various buildings which are used to produce other products for consumption.
    a. Wealth inequality in the United States
    b. Capital intensive
    c. Capital deepening
    d. Capital goods

43. A _____ is an object whose consumption increases the utility of the consumer, for which the quantity demanded exceeds the quantity supplied at zero price. _____s are usually modeled as having diminishing marginal utility. The first individual purchase has high utility; the second has less.
    a. Pie method
    b. Composite good
    c. Merit good
    d. Good

Chapter 7. Production Economics

1. In microeconomics, _____ is quite simply the conversion of inputs into outputs. It is an economic process that uses resources to create a good or service that is suitable for exchange. This can include manufacturing, storing, shipping, and packaging.
   a. MET
   b. Solved
   c. Red Guards
   d. Production

2. _____s is the social science that studies the production, distribution, and consumption of goods and services. The term _____s comes from the Ancient Greek οἰκονομῐ́α from οἶκος (oikos, 'house') + νόμος (nomos, 'custom' or 'law'), hence 'rules of the house(hold)'. Current _____ models developed out of the broader field of political economy in the late 19th century, owing to a desire to use an empirical approach more akin to the physical sciences.
   a. Opportunity cost
   b. Energy economics
   c. Economic
   d. Inflation

3. _____ is the term denoting either an entrance or changes which are inserted into a system and which activate/modify a process. It is an abstract concept, used in the modeling, system(s) design and system(s) exploitation. It is usually connected with other terms, e.g., _____ field, _____ variable, _____ parameter, _____ value, _____ signal, _____ device and _____ file.
   a. Input
   b. AD-IA Model
   c. ACCRA Cost of Living Index
   d. ACEA agreement

4. In economics, a _____ is a function that specifies the output of a firm, an industry, or an entire economy for all combinations of inputs. A meta-_____ compares the practice of the existing entities converting inputs X into output y to determine the most efficient practice _____ of the existing entities, whether the most efficient feasible practice production or the most efficient actual practice production. In either case, the maximum output of a technologically-determined production process is a mathematical function of input factors of production.
   a. Short-run
   b. Production function
   c. Constant elasticity of substitution
   d. Post-Fordism

5. In economics, the _____ functional form of production functions is widely used to represent the relationship of an output to inputs. It was proposed by Knut Wicksell (1851-1926), and tested against statistical evidence by Charles Cobb and Paul Douglas in 1900-1928.

Chapter 7. Production Economics

For production, the function is

$$Y = AL^{\alpha}K^{\beta},$$

where:

- Y = total production (the monetary value of all goods produced in a year)
- L = labor input
- K = capital input
- A = total factor productivity
- α and β are the output elasticities of labor and capital, respectively. These values are constants determined by available technology.

Output elasticity measures the responsiveness of output to a change in levels of either labor or capital used in production, ceteris paribus. For example if α = 0.15, a 1% increase in labor would lead to approximately a 0.15% increase in output.

a. Growth accounting
b. Social savings
c. Demand-pull theory
d. Cobb-Douglas

6. _____s are expenses that change in proportion to the activity of a business. In other words, _____ is the sum of marginal costs. It can also be considered normal costs.
   a. Variable cost
   b. Cost allocation
   c. Cost-Volume-Profit Analysis
   d. Quality costs

7. In economics, the _____ or marginal physical product is the extra output produced by one more unit of an input (for instance, the difference in output when a firm's labour is increased from five to six units.) Assuming that no other inputs to production change, the _____ of a given input (X) can be expressed as:

   _____ = ΔY/ΔX = (the change of Y)/(the change of X.)

   -
     -
       - Pending approval by Thomas Sowell***

In neoclassical economics, this is the mathematical derivative of the production function.... Note that the 'product' (Y) is typically defined ignoring external costs and benefits.

   a. Productive capacity
   b. Factor prices
   c. Labor problem
   d. Marginal product

8. In economics, the _____ is the idea that a nation is better off when it produces goods and services for which it has a comparative advantage.
   a. Law of comparative advantage
   b. Keynesian economics
   c. Recession
   d. Monopolistic competition

9. In economics, _____ refers to the ability of a person or a country to produce a particular good at a lower marginal cost and opportunity cost than another person or country. It is the ability to produce a product most efficiently given all the other products that could be produced. It can be contrasted with absolute advantage which refers to the ability of a person or a country to produce a particular good at a lower absolute cost than another.
   a. Hot money
   b. Comparative advantage
   c. Gravity model of trade
   d. Triffin dilemma

10. In economics, _____ refers to how the marginal contribution of a factor of production usually decreases as more of the factor is used. According to this relationship, in a production system with fixed and variable inputs, beyond some point, each additional unit of the variable input yields smaller and smaller increases in output. Conversely, producing one more unit of output costs more and more in variable inputs.
   a. Community property
   b. Diminishing returns
   c. Derivatives law
   d. Patent troll

11. In economics and business, a _____ is the effect that one user of a good or service has on the value of that product to other people.

Chapter 7. Production Economics

The classic example is the telephone. The more people own telephones, the more valuable the telephone is to each owner.

a. Pigou effect
b. Network effect
c. Penn effect
d. Cluster effect

12. In calculus, a function f defined on a subset of the real numbers with real values is called _____, if for all x and y such that x >≤ y one has f(x) >≤ f(y), so f preserves the order. In layman's terms, the sign of the slope is always positive (the curve tending upwards) or zero (i.e., non-decreasing, or asymptotic, or depicted as a horizontal, flat line) Likewise, a function is called monotonically decreasing (non-increasing) if, whenever x >≤ y, then f(x) >≥ f(y), so it reverses the order.
    a. Monotonic
    b. 100-year flood
    c. 1921 recession
    d. 130-30 fund

13. _____ or the economics of information is a branch of microeconomic theory that studies how information affects an economy and economic decisions. Information has special characteristics. It is easy to create but hard to trust.
    a. Information economics
    b. ACEA agreement
    c. AD-IA Model
    d. ACCRA Cost of Living Index

14. The _____ of a variable factor of Production identifies what outputs are possible using various levels of the variable input. This can be displayed in either a chart that lists the output level corresponding to various levels of input, or a graph that summarizes the data into a '_____ curve'. The diagram shows a typical _____ curve. In this example, output increases as more inputs are employed up until point A. The maximum output possible with this Production process is Qm. (If there are other inputs used in the process, they are assumed to be fixed).
    a. Tightness
    b. Convexity
    c. Total product
    d. Consequence

15. In economics, _____ is the ratio of the percent change in one variable to the percent change in another variable. It is a tool for measuring the responsiveness of a function to changes in parameters in a relative way. Commonly analyzed are _____ of substitution, price and wealth.

Chapter 7. Production Economics

   a. ACEA agreement
   b. Elasticity of demand
   c. ACCRA Cost of Living Index
   d. Elasticity

16. _____ in economics and business is the result of an exchange and from that trade we assign a numerical monetary value to a good, service or asset. If Alice trades Bob 4 apples for an orange, the _____ of an orange is 4 apples. Inversely, the _____ of an apple is 1/4 oranges.
   a. Price
   b. Price book
   c. Premium pricing
   d. Price war

17. In microeconomics, _____ is the extra revenue that an additional unit of product will bring. It is the additional income from selling one more unit of a good; sometimes equal to price. It can also be described as the change in total revenue/change in number of units sold.
   a. Long term
   b. Market demand schedule
   c. Reservation price
   d. Marginal revenue

18. The marginal revenue productivity theory of wages, also referred to as the _____ of labor, is the change in total revenue earned by a firm that results from employing one more unit of labor. It is a neoclassical model that determines, under some conditions, the optimal number of workers to employ at an exogenously determined market wage rate.

The _____ of a worker is equal to the product of the marginal product of labor (MP) and the marginal revenue (MR), given by MR×MP = _____.

   a. Marginal revenue productivity theory of wages
   b. Coal depletion
   c. Real prices and ideal prices
   d. Marginal revenue product

19. _____ or national income by type of income is a measure of national income or output based on the cost of factors of production, instead of market prices. This allows the effect of any subsidy or indirect tax to be removed from the final measure.

Chapter 7. Production Economics

a. Corporate synergy
b. Gross regional domestic product
c. Factor cost
d. Lehman scale

20. In economics, an _____ is a contour line drawn through the set of points at which the same quantity of output is produced while changing the quantities of two or more inputs. While an indifference curve helps to answer the utility-maximizing problem of consumers, the _____ deals with the cost-minimization problem of producers. _____s are typically drawn on capital-labor graphs, showing the tradeoff between capital and labor in the production function, and the decreasing marginal returns of both inputs.

a. Underinvestment employment relationship
b. Economic production quantity
c. Economies of scale
d. Isoquant

21. In economics, the _____ or the Technical Rate of Substitution (TRS) is the amount by which the quantity of one input has to be reduced (− Δx$_2$) when one extra unit of another input is used (Δx$_1$ = 1), so that output remains constant ($y = \bar{y}$.)

$$MRTS(x_1, x_2) = \frac{\Delta x_2}{\Delta x_1} = -\frac{MP_1}{MP_2}$$

where MP$_1$ and MP$_2$ are the marginal products of input 1 and input 2, respectively.

Along an isoquant, the MRTS shows the rate at which one input (e.g. capital or labor) may be substituted for another, while maintaining the same level of output.

a. Producer surplus
b. Pork cycle
c. Household production function
d. Marginal rate of technical substitution

22. _____ is a situation in which the limited resources of a firm are allocated in accordance with the wishes of consumers. An allocatively efficient economy produces an 'optimal mix' of commodities. A firm is allocatively efficient when its price is equal to its marginal costs (that is, P = MC) in a perfect market.

a. ACEA agreement
b. Economic efficiency
c. ACCRA Cost of Living Index
d. Allocative efficiency

23. In economics, _____ and economies of scale are related terms that describe what happens as the scale of production increases. They are different terms and should not be used interchangeably.

_____ refers to a technical property of production that examines changes in output subsequent to a proportional change in all inputs (where all inputs increase by a constant factor.)

a. Customer equity
b. Constant returns to scale
c. Necessity good
d. Returns to scale

Chapter 8. Cost Analysis

1. _____ or economic opportunity loss is the value of the next best alternative foregone as the result of making a decision. _____ analysis is an important part of a company's decision-making processes but is not treated as an actual cost in any financial statement. The next best thing that a person can engage in is referred to as the _____ of doing the best thing and ignoring the next best thing to be done.
   a. Industrial organization
   b. Economic ideology
   c. Economic
   d. Opportunity cost

2. _____s is the social science that studies the production, distribution, and consumption of goods and services. The term _____s comes from the Ancient Greek oá¼°κονομῖα from oá¼¶κος (oikos, 'house') + vÏŒμος (nomos, 'custom' or 'law'), hence 'rules of the house(hold)'. Current _____ models developed out of the broader field of political economy in the late 19th century, owing to a desire to use an empirical approach more akin to the physical sciences.
   a. Energy economics
   b. Inflation
   c. Opportunity cost
   d. Economic

3. The _____ of a decision depends on both the cost of the alternative chosen and the benefit that the best alternative would have provided if chosen. _____ differs from accounting cost because it includes opportunity cost.
   a. Isocost
   b. Inventory analysis
   c. Epstein-Zin preferences
   d. Economic cost

4. The term _____ has three unrelated technical definitions, and is also used in a variety of non-technical ways.

- In financial economics, it refers to any asset used to make money, as opposed to assets used for personal enjoyment or consumption. This is an important distinction because two people can disagree sharply about the value of personal assets, one person might think a sports car is more valuable than a pickup truck, another person might have the opposite taste. But if an asset is held for the purpose of making money, taste has nothing to do with it, only differences of opinion about how much money the asset will produce. With the further assumption that people agree on the probability distribution of future cash flows, it is possible to have an objective _____ pricing model. Even without the assumption of agreement, it is possible to set rational limits on _____ value.
- In governmental accounting, it is defined as any asset used in operations with an initial useful life extending beyond one reporting period. Generally, government managers have a 'stewardship' duty to maintain _____s under their control. See International Public Sector Accounting Standards for details.
- In US tax accounting, it is defined as any property other than a list of exceptions. The main exceptions are anything held for sale, and any real estate or depreciable property used in business. Almost everything you own and use for personal purposes, pleasure or investment is a _____. If something is a _____ for tax purposes, gains or losses on sale or disposition are capital gains or capital losses. For individuals, however, capital losses on property held for personal use are generally not deductible. See the IRS publication Tax Facts about Capital Gains and Losses for details.

A well-known financial accounting textbook advises that the term be avoided except in tax accounting because it is used in so many different senses, not all of them well-defined. For example it is often used as a synonym for fixed assets or for investments in securities.

A common non-technical usage occurs when people ask that employees or the environment or something else be treated as a _____.

a. Capital asset
b. Consumption beta
c. Mid price
d. Dynamic asset allocation

5. _____ is a term used in accounting, economics and finance to spread the cost of an asset over the span of several years.

In simple words we can say that _____ is the reduction in the value of an asset due to usage, passage of time, wear and tear, technological outdating or obsolescence, depletion, inadequacy, rot, rust, decay or other such factors.

In accounting, _____ is a term used to describe any method of attributing the historical or purchase cost of an asset across its useful life, roughly corresponding to normal wear and tear.

Chapter 8. Cost Analysis

a. Net income per employee
b. Depreciation
c. Historical cost
d. Salvage value

6. In business and accounting, _____ are everything of value that is owned by a person or company. It is a claim on the property your income of a borrower. The balance sheet of a firm records the monetary value of the _____ owned by the firm.
    a. ACCRA Cost of Living Index
    b. Amortization schedule
    c. ACEA agreement
    d. Assets

7. In economics, _____ are business expenses that are not dependent on the activities of the business They tend to be time-related, such as salaries or rents being paid per month. This is in contrast to variable costs, which are volume-related (and are paid per quantity.)

In management accounting, _____ are defined as expenses that do not change in proportion to the activity of a business, within the relevant period or scale of production.

   a. Fixed costs
   b. Cost of poor quality
   c. Cost-Volume-Profit Analysis
   d. Quality costs

8. In economics, the concept of the _____ refers to the decision-making time frame of a firm in which at least one factor of production is fixed. Costs which are fixed in the _____ have no impact on a firms decisions. For example a firm can raise output by increasing the amount of labour through overtime.
   a. Hicks-neutral technical change
   b. Short-run
   c. Product Pipeline
   d. Productivity model

9. In economics, and cost accounting, _____ describes the total economic cost of production and is made up of variable costs, which vary according to the quantity of a good produced and include inputs such as labor and raw materials, plus fixed costs, which are independent of the quantity of a good produced and include inputs (capital) that cannot be varied in the short term, such as buildings and machinery. _____ in economics includes the total opportunity cost of each factor of production in addition to fixed and variable costs.

Chapter 8. Cost Analysis

The rate at which _____ changes as the amount produced changes is called marginal cost.

a. 130-30 fund
b. 100-year flood
c. 1921 recession
d. Total Cost

10. _____s are expenses that change in proportion to the activity of a business. In other words, _____ is the sum of marginal costs. It can also be considered normal costs.
a. Variable cost
b. Cost-Volume-Profit Analysis
c. Cost allocation
d. Quality costs

11. In economics, _____ is equal to total cost divided by the number of goods produced (the output quantity, Q.) It is also equal to the sum of average variable costs (total variable costs divided by Q) plus average fixed costs (total fixed costs divided by Q.) _____s may be dependent on the time period considered (increasing production may be expensive or impossible in the short term, for example.)
a. Average fixed cost
b. Average cost
c. Explicit cost
d. Average variable cost

12. In economics and finance, _____ is the change in total cost that arises when the quantity produced changes by one unit. It is the cost of producing one more unit of a good. Mathematically, the _____ function is expressed as the first derivative of the total cost (TC) function with respect to quantity (Q.)
a. Quality costs
b. Variable cost
c. Khozraschyot
d. Marginal cost

13. In microeconomics, _____ is quite simply the conversion of inputs into outputs. It is an economic process that uses resources to create a good or service that is suitable for exchange. This can include manufacturing, storing, shipping, and packaging.

Chapter 8. Cost Analysis

a. Red Guards
b. Solved
c. MET
d. Production

14. In economic models, the _____ time frame assumes no fixed factors of production. Firms can enter or leave the marketplace, and the cost (and availability) of land, labor, raw materials, and capital goods can be assumed to vary. In contrast, in the short-run time frame, certain factors are assumed to be fixed, because there is not sufficient time for them to change.
    a. Price/performance ratio
    b. Long-run
    c. Diseconomies of scale
    d. Productivity world

15. _____ is a concept in economics which refers to the extent to which an enterprise or a nation actually uses its installed productive capacity. Thus, it refers to the relationship between actual output that 'is' produced with the installed equipment and the potential output which 'could' be produced with it, if capacity was fully used.

If market demand grows, _____ will rise.

    a. Diseconomies of scale
    b. Marginal product of labor
    c. Long-run
    d. Capacity utilization

16. An example of _____ is when a company is cut in size but the remaining firms still hold the same amount of final output. Therefore the company has become more efficient in production and has experienced _____.the internal part of the business expands enabling the business to make higher profits.

Six main types of _____ can be defined.

    a. ACCRA Cost of Living Index
    b. AD-IA Model
    c. ACEA agreement
    d. Internal economies of scale

17. _____, in microeconomics, are the cost advantages that a business obtains due to expansion. They are factors that cause a producere;s average cost per unit to fall as scale is increased. _____ is a long run concept and refers to reductions in unit cost as the size of a facility, or scale, increases.

  a. Economic production quantity
  b. Isoquant
  c. Underinvestment employment relationship
  d. Economies of scale

18. _____ are the forces that cause larger firms to produce goods and services at increased per-unit costs. They are less well known than what economists have long understood as 'economies of scale', the forces which enable larger firms to produce goods and services at reduced per-unit costs.

Some of the forces which cause a diseconomy of scale are listed below:

Ideally, all employees of a firm would have one-on-one communication with each other so they know exactly what the other workers are doing.

  a. Marginal physical product
  b. Factors of production
  c. Diseconomies of scale
  d. Productive capacity

19. In economics, the _____ functional form of production functions is widely used to represent the relationship of an output to inputs. It was proposed by Knut Wicksell (1851-1926), and tested against statistical evidence by Charles Cobb and Paul Douglas in 1900-1928.

For production, the function is

$$Y = AL^{\alpha}K^{\beta},$$

where:

- Y = total production (the monetary value of all goods produced in a year)
- L = labor input
- K = capital input
- A = total factor productivity
- α and β are the output elasticities of labor and capital, respectively. These values are constants determined by available technology.

Chapter 8. Cost Analysis

Output elasticity measures the responsiveness of output to a change in levels of either labor or capital used in production, ceteris paribus. For example if α = 0.15, a 1% increase in labor would lead to approximately a 0.15% increase in output.

a. Demand-pull theory
b. Growth accounting
c. Social savings
d. Cobb-Douglas

20. In economics, a _____ is a function that specifies the output of a firm, an industry, or an entire economy for all combinations of inputs. A meta-_____ compares the practice of the existing entities converting inputs X into output y to determine the most efficient practice _____ of the existing entities, whether the most efficient feasible practice production or the most efficient actual practice production. In either case, the maximum output of a technologically-determined production process is a mathematical function of input factors of production.

a. Constant elasticity of substitution
b. Production function
c. Short-run
d. Post-Fordism

21. In calculus, a function f defined on a subset of the real numbers with real values is called _____, if for all x and y such that x >≤ y one has f(x) >≤ f(y), so f preserves the order. In layman's terms, the sign of the slope is always positive (the curve tending upwards) or zero (i.e., non-decreasing, or asymptotic, or depicted as a horizontal, flat line) Likewise, a function is called monotonically decreasing (non-increasing) if, whenever x >≤ y, then f(x) >≥ f(y), so it reverses the order.

a. 1921 recession
b. 100-year flood
c. 130-30 fund
d. Monotonic

Chapter 9. Applications of Cost Theory

1. In economics, the concept of the _____ refers to the decision-making time frame of a firm in which at least one factor of production is fixed. Costs which are fixed in the _____ have no impact on a firms decisions. For example a firm can raise output by increasing the amount of labour through overtime.
   a. Product Pipeline
   b. Productivity model
   c. Hicks-neutral technical change
   d. Short-run

2. In economic models, the _____ time frame assumes no fixed factors of production. Firms can enter or leave the marketplace, and the cost (and availability) of land, labor, raw materials, and capital goods can be assumed to vary. In contrast, in the short-run time frame, certain factors are assumed to be fixed, because there is not sufficient time for them to change.
   a. Price/performance ratio
   b. Long-run
   c. Diseconomies of scale
   d. Productivity world

3. In economics and business, specifically cost accounting, the _____ point (BEP) is the point at which cost or expenses and revenue are equal: there is no net loss or gain, and one has 'broken even'. A profit or a loss has not been made, although opportunity costs have been paid, and capital has received the risk-adjusted, expected return.

   For example, if the business sells less than 200 tables each month, it will make a loss, if it sells more, it will be a profit.

   a. Break-even
   b. Buffer stock scheme
   c. Small numbers game
   d. Nonmarket

4. The break-even point for a product is the point where total revenue received equals the total costs associated with the sale of the product (TR=TC.) A break-even point is typically calculated in order for businesses to determine if it would be profitable to sell a proposed product, as opposed to attempting to modify an existing product instead so it can be made lucrative. _____ can also be used to analyse the potential profitability of an expenditure in a sales-based business.
   a. Break even analysis
   b. Competitor indexing
   c. Flat rate
   d. Price

Chapter 9. Applications of Cost Theory

5. In cost-volume-profit analysis, a form of management accounting, _____ is the marginal profit per unit sale. It is a useful quantity in carrying out various calculations, and can be used as a measure of operating leverage.

The Total _____ is Total Revenue (TR, or Sales) minus Total Variable Cost (TVC):

TContribution margin = TR >− TVC

The Unit _____ (C) is Unit Revenue (Price, P) minus Unit Variable Cost (V):

C = P >− V

The _____ Ratio is the percentage of Contribution over Total Revenue, which can be calculated from the unit contribution over unit price or total contribution over Total Revenue:

For instance, if the price is $10 and the unit variable cost is $2, then the unit _____ is $8, and the _____ ratio is $8/$10 = 80%.

a. 100-year flood
b. Contribution margin
c. 1921 recession
d. 130-30 fund

6. The _____ is a measure of how revenue growth translates into growth in operating income. It is a measure of leverage, and of how risky (volatile) a company's operating income is.

There are various measures of _____, which can be interpreted analogously to financial leverage.

a. Operating margin
b. Upside potential ratio
c. Invested Capital
d. Operating leverage

7. _____ is a step in a risk management process. _____ is the determination of quantitative or qualitative value of risk related to a concrete situation and a recognized threat (also called hazard.) Quantitative _____ requires calculations of two components of risk: R, the magnitude of the potential loss L, and the probability p that the loss will occur.

a. 100-year flood
b. Risk assessment
c. 1921 recession
d. 130-30 fund

8. _____, in marketing, manufacturing, call centres and management, is the use of flexible computer-aided manufacturing systems to produce custom output. Those systems combine the low unit costs of mass production processes with the flexibility of individual customization.

'_____' is the new frontier in business competition for both manufacturing and service industries.

a. 100-year flood
b. 1921 recession
c. 130-30 fund
d. Mass customization

Chapter 10. Prices, Output, and Strategy: Pure and Monopolistic Competition

1. _____ is a common market structure where many competing producers sell products that are differentiated from one another (ie. the products are substitutes, but are not exactly alike.) Many markets are monopolistically competitive, common examples include the markets for restaurants, cereal, clothing, shoes and service industries in large cities.

   a. Mathematical economics
   b. Financial crisis
   c. Perfect competition
   d. Monopolistic competition

2. _____ is the a method of technical and economic research of the systems for purpose to optimize a parity between system's consumer functions or properties and expenses to achieve those functions or properties.

This methodology for continuous perfection of production, industrial technologies, organizational structures was developed by Juryj Sobolev in 1948 at the 'Perm telephone factory'

- 1948 Juryj Sobolev - the first success in application of a method analysis at the 'Perm telephone factory' .
- 1949 - the first application for the invention as result of use of the new method.

Today in economically developed countries practically each enterprise or the company use methodology of the kind of functional-cost analysis as a practice of the quality management, most full satisfying to principles of standards of series ISO 9000.

- Interest of consumer not in products itself, but the advantage which it will receive from its usage.
- The consumer aspires to reduce his expenses
- Functions needed by consumer can be executed in the various ways, and, hence, with various efficiency and expenses. Among possible alternatives of realization of functions exist such in which the parity of quality and the price is the optimal for the consumer.

The goal of _____ is achievement of the highest consumer satisfaction of production at simultaneous decrease in all kinds of industrial expenses Classical _____ has three English synonyms - Value Engineering, Value Management, Value Analysis.

   a. Willingness to pay
   b. Staple financing
   c. Monopoly wage
   d. Function cost analysis

3. In marketing, _____ is the process of distinguishing the differences of a product or offering from others, to make it more attractive to a particular target market. This involves differentiating it from competitors' products as well as one's own product offerings.

Differentiation is a source of competitive advantage.

a. Market segment
b. Technology acceptance model
c. Pricing science
d. Product differentiation

4.

_____ is, in very basic words, a position a firm occupies against its competitors.

According to Michael Porter, the three methods for creating a sustainable _____ are through:

1. Cost leadership - Cost advantage occurs when a firm delivers the same services as its competitors but at a lower cost;

2. Differentiation - Differentiation advantage occurs when a firm delivers greater services for the same price of its competitors. They are collectively known as positional advantages because they denote the firm's position in its industry as a leader in either superior services or cost;

3. Focus (economics) - A focused approach requires the firm to concentrate on a narrow, exclusive competitive segment (market niche), hoping to achieve a local rather than industry wide _____. There are cost focus seekers, who aim to obtain a local cost advantage over competition and differentiation focuser, who are looking for a local difference.

a. National Diamond
b. Six Forces Model
c. Chaos theory in organizational development
d. Competitive advantage

5. _____ or the economics of information is a branch of microeconomic theory that studies how information affects an economy and economic decisions. Information has special characteristics. It is easy to create but hard to trust.
a. ACEA agreement
b. ACCRA Cost of Living Index
c. Information economics
d. AD-IA Model

6. _____s is the social science that studies the production, distribution, and consumption of goods and services. The term _____s comes from the Ancient Greek οἰκονομία from οἶκος (oikos, 'house') + νόμος (nomos, 'custom' or 'law'), hence 'rules of the house(hold)'. Current _____ models developed out of the broader field of political economy in the late 19th century, owing to a desire to use an empirical approach more akin to the physical sciences.

Chapter 10. Prices, Output, and Strategy: Pure and Monopolistic Competition

a. Inflation
b. Energy economics
c. Opportunity cost
d. Economic

7. In competition law the _____ defines the market in which one or more goods compete. Therefore, the _____ defines whether two or more products can be considered substitute goods and whether they constitute a particular and separate market for competition analysis.

The _____ combines the product market and the geographic market, defined as follows:

1. A relevant product market comprises all those products and/or services which are regarded as interchangeable or substitutable by the consumer by reason of the products' characteristics, their prices and their intended use;
2. A relevant geographic market comprises the area in which the firms concerned are involved in the supply of products or services and in which the conditions of competition are sufficiently homogeneous.

The notion of _____ is used in order to identify the products and undertakings which are directly competing in a business. Therefore, the _____ is the market where the competition takes place.

a. Competition law
b. Relevant market
c. Community property
d. Greenfield agreement

8. In economics and business, specifically cost accounting, the _____ point (BEP) is the point at which cost or expenses and revenue are equal: there is no net loss or gain, and one has 'broken even'. A profit or a loss has not been made, although opportunity costs have been paid, and capital has received the risk-adjusted, expected return.

For example, if the business sells less than 200 tables each month, it will make a loss, if it sells more, it will be a profit.

a. Nonmarket
b. Small numbers game
c. Buffer stock scheme
d. Break-even

9. In economics and especially in the theory of competition, _____ are obstacles in the path of a firm that make it difficult to enter a given market.

Chapter 10. Prices, Output, and Strategy: Pure and Monopolistic Competition

_____ are the source of a firm's pricing power - the ability of a firm to raise prices without losing all its customers.

The term refers to hindrances that an individual may face while trying to gain entrance into a profession or trade.

a. Limit price
b. Group boycott
c. Social dumping
d. Barriers to entry

10. _____, in strategic management and marketing is, according to Carlton O'Neal, the percentage or proportion of the total available market or market segment that is being serviced by a company. It can be expressed as a company's sales revenue (from that market) divided by the total sales revenue available in that market. It can also be expressed as a company's unit sales volume (in a market) divided by the total volume of units sold in that market.

a. Customer to customer
b. Product differentiation
c. Market share
d. Pricing science

11. In economics, _____ describes the state of a market with respect to competition.

- Perfect competition, in which the market consists of a very large number of firms producing a homogeneous product.
- Monopolistic competition where there are a large number of independent firms which have a very small proportion of the market share.
- Oligopoly, in which a market is dominated by a small number of firms which own more than 40% of the market share.
- Oligopsony, a market dominated by many sellers and a few buyers.
- Monopoly, where there is only one provider of a product or service.
- Natural monopoly, a monopoly in which economies of scale cause efficiency to increase continuously with the size of the firm. A firm is a natural monopoly if it is able to serve the entire market demand at a lower cost than any combination of two or more smaller, more specialized firms.
- Monopsony, when there is only one buyer in a market.

The imperfectly competitive structure is quite identical to the realistic market conditions where some monopolistic competitors, monopolists, oligopolists, and duopolists exist and dominate the market conditions. The elements of _____ include the number and size distribution of firms, entry conditions, and the extent of differentiation.

These somewhat abstract concerns tend to determine some but not all details of a specific concrete market system where buyers and sellers actually meet and commit to trade.

Chapter 10. Prices, Output, and Strategy: Pure and Monopolistic Competition

a. Human capital
b. Market structure
c. Monopolistic competition
d. Labour economics

12. In economics, a _____ exists when a specific individual or enterprise has sufficient control over a particular product or service to determine significantly the terms on which other individuals shall have access to it. Monopolies are thus characterized by a lack of economic competition for the good or service that they provide and a lack of viable substitute goods. The verb 'monopolize' refers to the process by which a firm gains persistently greater market share than what is expected under perfect competition.

a. 130-30 fund
b. Monopoly
c. 100-year flood
d. 1921 recession

13. An _____ is a market form in which a market or industry is dominated by a small number of sellers (oligopolists.) Because there are few participants in this type of market, each oligopolist is aware of the actions of the others. The decisions of one firm influence, and are influenced by, the decisions of other firms.

a. Oligopoly
b. ACEA agreement
c. Oligopsony
d. ACCRA Cost of Living Index

14. In economics, _____ is the ratio of the percent change in one variable to the percent change in another variable. It is a tool for measuring the responsiveness of a function to changes in parameters in a relative way. Commonly analyzed are _____ of substitution, price and wealth.

a. Elasticity of demand
b. ACCRA Cost of Living Index
c. ACEA agreement
d. Elasticity

15. In economics, an _____ is a product or service where product characteristics such as quality or price are difficult to observe in advance, but these characteristics can be ascertained upon consumption. The concept is originally due to Philip Nelson, who contrasted an _____ with a search good.

_____s pose difficulties for consumers in accurately making consumption choices.

a. Independent goods
b. Experience good
c. Export-oriented
d. Information good

16. A _____ is an object whose consumption increases the utility of the consumer, for which the quantity demanded exceeds the quantity supplied at zero price. _____s are usually modeled as having diminishing marginal utility. The first individual purchase has high utility; the second has less.
   a. Composite good
   b. Pie method
   c. Merit good
   d. Good

17. In economics, a _____ is a product or service with features and characteristics easily evaluated before purchase. In a distinction originally due to Philip Nelson, a _____ is contrasted with an experience good.

_____s are more subject to substitution and price competition, as consumers can easily verify the price of the product and alternatives at other outlets and make sure that the products are comparable.

   a. Luxury good
   b. Search good
   c. Superior goods
   d. Substitute good

18. _____, anti-selection insurance, statistics, and risk management. It refers to a market process in which 'bad' results occur when buyers and sellers have asymmetric information (i.e. access to different information): the 'bad' products or customers are more likely to be selected. A bank that sets one price for all its checking account customers runs the risk of being adversely selected against by its low-balance, high-activity (and hence least profitable) customers.
   a. AD-IA Model
   b. ACEA agreement
   c. ACCRA Cost of Living Index
   d. Adverse selection

19. _____ in economics and business is the result of an exchange and from that trade we assign a numerical monetary value to a good, service or asset. If Alice trades Bob 4 apples for an orange, the _____ of an orange is 4 apples. Inversely, the _____ of an apple is 1/4 oranges.

Chapter 10. Prices, Output, and Strategy: Pure and Monopolistic Competition

a. Price war
b. Price book
c. Premium pricing
d. Price

20. In business and accounting, _____ are everything of value that is owned by a person or company. It is a claim on the property your income of a borrower. The balance sheet of a firm records the monetary value of the _____ owned by the firm.
   a. Assets
   b. ACCRA Cost of Living Index
   c. ACEA agreement
   d. Amortization schedule

21. _____ is a term related to the inter-party relationships of a transaction. It has been extensively studied in a variety of management and economics areas such as marketing, accounting, organizational behavior and management information systems.

The concept of _____ is closely related to that of opportunism.

   a. Ask price
   b. Asset specificity
   c. Indexation
   d. Investment protection

Chapter 11. Price and Output Determination: Monopoly and Dominant Firms

1. In economics, a _____ exists when a specific individual or enterprise has sufficient control over a particular product or service to determine significantly the terms on which other individuals shall have access to it. Monopolies are thus characterized by a lack of economic competition for the good or service that they provide and a lack of viable substitute goods. The verb 'monopolize' refers to the process by which a firm gains persistently greater market share than what is expected under perfect competition.
    a. Monopoly
    b. 130-30 fund
    c. 1921 recession
    d. 100-year flood

2. _____ in economics and business is the result of an exchange and from that trade we assign a numerical monetary value to a good, service or asset. If Alice trades Bob 4 apples for an orange, the _____ of an orange is 4 apples. Inversely, the _____ of an apple is 1/4 oranges.
    a. Price book
    b. Premium pricing
    c. Price war
    d. Price

3. In economics, a firm is said to reap monopoly profits when a lack of viable market competition allows it to set its prices above the equilibrium price for a good or service without losing profits to competitors. Monopoly profit is a type of economic profit, that is, it is a profit greater than the normal profit that is typical in a perfectly competitive industry. The resulting price is known as the _____.
    a. Gross national income
    b. Payment schedule
    c. Gross Dealer Concession
    d. Monopoly Price

4. In economics, _____ is the ability of a firm to alter the market price of a good or service. A firm with _____ can raise prices without losing all customers to competitors.

    When a firm has _____ it faces a downward-sloping demand curve.

    a. Price makers
    b. Revenue-cap regulation
    c. Market power
    d. Pacman conjecture

5. In economics and business, a _____ is the effect that one user of a good or service has on the value of that product to other people.

Chapter 11. Price and Output Determination: Monopoly and Dominant Firms

The classic example is the telephone. The more people own telephones, the more valuable the telephone is to each owner.

a. Pigou effect
b. Cluster effect
c. Penn effect
d. Network effect

6. In calculus, a function f defined on a subset of the real numbers with real values is called _____, if for all x and y such that x >≤ y one has f(x) >≤ f(y), so f preserves the order. In layman's terms, the sign of the slope is always positive (the curve tending upwards) or zero (i.e., non-decreasing, or asymptotic, or depicted as a horizontal, flat line) Likewise, a function is called monotonically decreasing (non-increasing) if, whenever x >≤ y, then f(x) >≥ f(y), so it reverses the order.

a. 130-30 fund
b. 1921 recession
c. Monotonic
d. 100-year flood

7. In economics, a firm is said to reap _____s when a lack of viable market competition allows it to set its prices above the equilibrium price for a good or service without losing profits to competitors. _____ is a type of economic profit, that is, it is a profit greater than the normal profit that is typical in a perfectly competitive industry. The resulting price is known as the monopoly price.

a. Borrowing base
b. First-price sealed-bid auction
c. Cleanup clause
d. Monopoly profit

8. In economics, _____ is the process by which a firm determines the price and output level that returns the greatest profit. There are several approaches to this problem. The total revenue--total cost method relies on the fact that profit equals revenue minus cost, and the marginal revenue--marginal cost method is based on the fact that total profit in a perfectly competitive market reaches its maximum point where marginal revenue equals marginal cost.

a. Profit margin
b. 100-year flood
c. Normal profit
d. Profit maximization

Chapter 11. Price and Output Determination: Monopoly and Dominant Firms

9. _____ is defined as the measure of responsiveness in the quantity demanded for a commodity as a result of change in price of the same commodity. It is a measure of how consumers react to a change in price. In other words, it is percentage change in quantity demanded as per the percentage change in price of the same commodity.
   a. 100-year flood
   b. 130-30 fund
   c. 1921 recession
   d. Price elasticity of demand

10. Economics:

   - _____, the desire to own something and the ability to pay for it
   - _____ curve, a graphic representation of a _____ schedule
   - _____ deposit, the money in checking accounts
   - _____ pull theory, the theory that inflation occurs when _____ for goods and services exceeds existing supplies
   - _____ schedule, a table that lists the quantity of a good a person will buy it each different price
   - _____ side economics, the school of economics at believes government spending and tax cuts open economy by raising _____

   a. Production
   b. McKesson ' Robbins scandal
   c. Variability
   d. Demand

11. In economics, _____ is the ratio of the percent change in one variable to the percent change in another variable. It is a tool for measuring the responsiveness of a function to changes in parameters in a relative way. Commonly analyzed are _____ of substitution, price and wealth.
   a. ACCRA Cost of Living Index
   b. Elasticity of demand
   c. Elasticity
   d. ACEA agreement

12. Price _____ is defined as the measure of responsiveness in the quantity demanded for a commodity as a result of change in price of the same commodity. It is a measure of how consumers react to a change in price. In other words, it is percentage change in quantity demanded by the percentage change in price of the same commodity.

Chapter 11. Price and Output Determination: Monopoly and Dominant Firms 75

a. ACEA agreement
b. Elasticity
c. ACCRA Cost of Living Index
d. Elasticity of demand

13. In cost-volume-profit analysis, a form of management accounting, _____ is the marginal profit per unit sale. It is a useful quantity in carrying out various calculations, and can be used as a measure of operating leverage.

The Total _____ is Total Revenue (TR, or Sales) minus Total Variable Cost (TVC):

    TContribution margin = TR >− TVC

The Unit _____ (C) is Unit Revenue (Price, P) minus Unit Variable Cost (V):

    C = P >− V

The _____ Ratio is the percentage of Contribution over Total Revenue, which can be calculated from the unit contribution over unit price or total contribution over Total Revenue:

For instance, if the price is $10 and the unit variable cost is $2, then the unit _____ is $8, and the _____ ratio is $8/$10 = 80%.

a. 130-30 fund
b. 1921 recession
c. 100-year flood
d. Contribution margin

14. _____ is a financial ratio used to assess the profitability of a firm's core activities, excluding fixed costs.

The general calculation is:

$$\text{Gross profit margin} = \frac{\text{Revenue} - \text{Cost of Sales}}{\text{Revenue}}$$

The _____ is related to the net profit margin, which assesses the profitability of an organization after including fixed costs.

_____ indicates the relationship between net sales revenue and the cost of goods sold.

a. Bookrunner
b. Hot equity periods
c. Gross profit margin
d. Participating preferred stock

15. _____, net margin, net _____ or net profit ratio all refer to a measure of profitability. It is calculated by finding the net profit as a percentage of the revenue.

$$\text{Net profit margin} = \frac{\text{Net profit (after taxes)}}{\text{Revenue}} \times 100$$

The _____ is mostly used for internal comparison.

a. Profit maximization
b. Normal profit
c. 100-year flood
d. Profit margin

16. A limit price is the price set by a monopolist to discourage economic entry into a market, and is illegal in many countries. The limit price is the price that the entrant would face upon entering as long as the incumbent firm did not decrease output. The limit price is often lower than the average cost of production or just low enough to make entering not profitable. The quantity produced by the incumbent firm to act as a deterrent to entry is usually larger than would be optimal for a monopolist, but might still produce higher economic profits than would be earned under perfect competition. The problem with _____ as strategic behavior is that once the entrant has entered the market, the quantity used as a threat to deter entry is no longer the incumbent firm's best response.

a. Conscious parallelism
b. Third line forcing
c. Predatory pricing
d. Limit pricing

17. _____ is one of the four Ps of the marketing mix. The other three aspects are product, promotion, and place. It is also a key variable in microeconomic price allocation theory.

a. Premium pricing
b. Guaranteed Maximum Price
c. Point of total assumption
d. Pricing

Chapter 11. Price and Output Determination: Monopoly and Dominant Firms

18. A public utility (usually just utility) is an organization that maintains the infrastructure for a public service (often also providing a service using that infrastructure.) _____ are subject to forms of public control and regulation ranging from local community-based groups to state-wide government monopolies. Common arguments in favor of regulation include the desire to control market power, facilitate competition, promote investment or system expansion, or stabilize markets.
   a. 100-year flood
   b. 1921 recession
   c. 130-30 fund
   d. Public utilities

19. In economics, a _____ occurs when, due to the economies of scale of a particular industry, the maximum efficiency of production and distribution is realized through a single supplier.

   Natural monopolies arise where the largest supplier in an industry, often the first supplier in a market, has an overwhelming cost advantage over other actual or potential competitors. This tends to be the case in industries where capital costs predominate, creating economies of scale which are large in relation to the size of the market, and hence high barriers to entry; examples include water services and electricity.

   a. Collective goods
   b. Privatizing profits and socializing losses
   c. Common-pool resource
   d. Natural monopoly

20. _____s is the social science that studies the production, distribution, and consumption of goods and services. The term _____s comes from the Ancient Greek oá¼°κονομῖα from oá¼¶κος (oikos, 'house') + vÏŒμος (nomos, 'custom' or 'law'), hence 'rules of the house(hold)'. Current _____ models developed out of the broader field of political economy in the late 19th century, owing to a desire to use an empirical approach more akin to the physical sciences.
   a. Opportunity cost
   b. Energy economics
   c. Inflation
   d. Economic

21. In economics, _____ is a measure of the relative satisfaction from consumption of various goods and services. Given this measure, one may speak meaningfully of increasing or decreasing _____, and thereby explain economic behavior in terms of attempts to increase one's _____. For illustrative purposes, changes in _____ are sometimes expressed in units called utils.

a. Utility function
b. Utility
c. Ordinal utility
d. Expected utility hypothesis

22. _____ is a pricing technique applied to public goods, which is a particular case of a Lindahl equilibrium. Instead of different demands for the same public good, we consider the demands for a public good in different periods of the day, month or year, then finding the optimal capacity (quantity supplied) and, afterwards, the optimal peak-load prices.

This has particular applications in public goods such as public urban transportation, where day demand (peak period) is usually much higher than night demand (off-peak period.)

a. Demand management
b. Cobra effect
c. Fiscal imbalance
d. Peak-load pricing

Chapter 12. Price and Output Determination: Oligopoly

1. An _____ is a market form in which a market or industry is dominated by a small number of sellers (oligopolists.) Because there are few participants in this type of market, each oligopolist is aware of the actions of the others. The decisions of one firm influence, and are influenced by, the decisions of other firms.
   a. ACEA agreement
   b. Oligopsony
   c. ACCRA Cost of Living Index
   d. Oligopoly

2. _____ in economics and business is the result of an exchange and from that trade we assign a numerical monetary value to a good, service or asset. If Alice trades Bob 4 apples for an orange, the _____ of an orange is 4 apples. Inversely, the _____ of an apple is 1/4 oranges.
   a. Premium pricing
   b. Price book
   c. Price
   d. Price war

3. In economics, _____ describes the state of a market with respect to competition.

   - Perfect competition, in which the market consists of a very large number of firms producing a homogeneous product.
   - Monopolistic competition where there are a large number of independent firms which have a very small proportion of the market share.
   - Oligopoly, in which a market is dominated by a small number of firms which own more than 40% of the market share.
   - Oligopsony, a market dominated by many sellers and a few buyers.
   - Monopoly, where there is only one provider of a product or service.
   - Natural monopoly, a monopoly in which economies of scale cause efficiency to increase continuously with the size of the firm. A firm is a natural monopoly if it is able to serve the entire market demand at a lower cost than any combination of two or more smaller, more specialized firms.
   - Monopsony, when there is only one buyer in a market.

   The imperfectly competitive structure is quite identical to the realistic market conditions where some monopolistic competitors, monopolists, oligopolists, and duopolists exist and dominate the market conditions. The elements of _____ include the number and size distribution of firms, entry conditions, and the extent of differentiation.

   These somewhat abstract concerns tend to determine some but not all details of a specific concrete market system where buyers and sellers actually meet and commit to trade.

   a. Monopolistic competition
   b. Labour economics
   c. Human capital
   d. Market structure

Chapter 12. Price and Output Determination: Oligopoly

4. _____, in strategic management and marketing is, according to Carlton O'Neal, the percentage or proportion of the total available market or market segment that is being serviced by a company. It can be expressed as a company's sales revenue (from that market) divided by the total sales revenue available in that market. It can also be expressed as a company's unit sales volume (in a market) divided by the total volume of units sold in that market.
   a. Customer to customer
   b. Market share
   c. Pricing science
   d. Product differentiation

5. _____ is an economic model used to describe an industry structure in which companies compete on the amount of output they will produce, which they decide on independently of each other and at the same time. It is named after Antoine Augustin Cournot (1801-1877) after he observed competition in a spring water duopoly. It has the following features:

   - There is more than one firm and all firms produce a homogeneous product, i.e. there is no product differentiation;
   - Firms do not cooperate, i.e. there is no collusion;
   - Firms have market power, i.e. each firm's output decision affects the good's price;
   - The number of firms is fixed;
   - Firms compete in quantities, and choose quantities simultaneously;
   - The firms are economically rational and act strategically, usually seeking to maximize profit given their competitors' decisions.

An essential assumption of this model is that each firm aims to maximize profits, based on the expectation that its own output decision will not have an effect on the decisions of its rivals. Price is a commonly known decreasing function of total output.

   a. 130-30 fund
   b. 100-year flood
   c. Cournot competition
   d. 1921 recession

6. A _____ is a counterfeit agreement among industries. It is an informal organization of producers that agree to coordinate prices and production. _____s usually occur in an oligopolistic industry, where there is a small number of sellers and usually involve homogeneous products.
   a. Shill
   b. 100-year flood
   c. Shanzhai
   d. Cartel

7. _____ is an agreement, usually secretive, which occurs between two or more persons to deceive, mislead or to obtain an objective forbidden by law typically involving fraud or gaining an unfair advantage. It is an agreement among firms to divide the market, set prices kickbacks, or misrepresenting the independence of the relationship between the colluding parties.' All acts effected by _____ are considered void.
   a. Dividing territories
   b. Net Book Agreement
   c. Bid rigging
   d. Collusion

8. In economics, _____ is the process by which a firm determines the price and output level that returns the greatest profit. There are several approaches to this problem. The total revenue--total cost method relies on the fact that profit equals revenue minus cost, and the marginal revenue--marginal cost method is based on the fact that total profit in a perfectly competitive market reaches its maximum point where marginal revenue equals marginal cost.
   a. 100-year flood
   b. Profit maximization
   c. Profit margin
   d. Normal profit

9. _____ is one of the four Ps of the marketing mix. The other three aspects are product, promotion, and place. It is also a key variable in microeconomic price allocation theory.
   a. Guaranteed Maximum Price
   b. Premium pricing
   c. Point of total assumption
   d. Pricing

10. The _____ curve theory is an economic theory regarding oligopoly and monopolistic competition. When it was created, the idea fundamentally challenged classical economic tenets such as efficient markets and rapidly-changing prices, ideas that underly basic supply and demand models. _____ was an initial attempt to explain sticky prices.
    a. Kinked demand curve
    b. Precautionary demand
    c. Marginal demand
    d. Kinked demand

11. The _____ theory is an economic theory regarding oligopoly and monopolistic competition. When it was created, the idea fundamentally challenged classical economic tenets such as efficient markets and rapidly-changing prices, ideas that underly basic supply and demand models. Kinked demand was an initial attempt to explain sticky prices.

a. Hicksian demand function
b. Kinked demand
c. Precautionary demand
d. Kinked demand curve

12. Economics:

    - _____,the desire to own something and the ability to pay for it
    - _____ curve,a graphic representation of a _____ schedule
    - _____ deposit, the money in checking accounts
    - _____ pull theory,the theory that inflation occurs when _____ for goods and services exceeds existing supplies
    - _____ schedule,a table that lists the quantity of a good a person will buy it each different price
    - _____ side economics,the school of economics at believes government spending and tax cuts open economy by raising _____

    a. McKesson ' Robbins scandal
    b. Demand
    c. Production
    d. Variability

13. In economics, the _____ can be defined as the graph depicting the relationship between the price of a certain commodity, and the amount of it that consumers are willing and able to purchase at that given price. It is a graphic representation of a demand schedule. The _____ for all consumers together follows from the _____ of every individual consumer: the individual demands at each price are added together.
    a. Wage curve
    b. Demand curve
    c. Cost curve
    d. Kuznets curve

14. _____ is a term used in business to indicate a state of intense competitive rivalry accompanied by a multi-lateral series of price reduction. One competitor will lower its price, then others will lower their prices to match. If one of them reduces their price again, a new round of reductions starts.
    a. Big ticket item
    b. Transactional Net Margin Method
    c. Discounts and allowances
    d. Price war

1. _____ is a branch of applied mathematics that is used in the social sciences (most notably economics), biology, engineering, political science, international relations, computer science, and philosophy. _____ attempts to mathematically capture behavior in strategic situations, in which an individual's success in making choices depends on the choices of others. While initially developed to analyze competitions in which one individual does better at another's expense (zero sum games), it has been expanded to treat a wide class of interactions, which are classified according to several criteria.

   a. Dollar auction
   b. Discriminatory price auction
   c. Proper equilibrium
   d. Game theory

2. In economics, _____ describes the state of a market with respect to competition.

   - Perfect competition, in which the market consists of a very large number of firms producing a homogeneous product.
   - Monopolistic competition where there are a large number of independent firms which have a very small proportion of the market share.
   - Oligopoly, in which a market is dominated by a small number of firms which own more than 40% of the market share.
   - Oligopsony, a market dominated by many sellers and a few buyers.
   - Monopoly, where there is only one provider of a product or service.
   - Natural monopoly, a monopoly in which economies of scale cause efficiency to increase continuously with the size of the firm. A firm is a natural monopoly if it is able to serve the entire market demand at a lower cost than any combination of two or more smaller, more specialized firms.
   - Monopsony, when there is only one buyer in a market.

   The imperfectly competitive structure is quite identical to the realistic market conditions where some monopolistic competitors, monopolists, oligopolists, and duopolists exist and dominate the market conditions. The elements of _____ include the number and size distribution of firms, entry conditions, and the extent of differentiation.

   These somewhat abstract concerns tend to determine some but not all details of a specific concrete market system where buyers and sellers actually meet and commit to trade.

   a. Human capital
   b. Market structure
   c. Monopolistic competition
   d. Labour economics

3. In game theory, _____ is a way of describing a game. Unlike extensive form, normal-form representations are not graphical per se, but rather represent the game by way of a matrix. While this approach can be of greater use in identifying strictly dominated strategies and Nash equilibria, some information is lost as compared to extensive-form representations.

a. 100-year flood
b. 130-30 fund
c. 1921 recession
d. Normal form

4. The concept was first developed in game theory and consequently zero-sum situations are often called _____s though this does not imply that the concept applies only to what are commonly referred to as games.

For 2-player finite _____s, the different game theoretic Solution concepts of Nash equilibrium, minimax, and maximin all give the same solution. In the solution, players play a mixed strategy.

a. Cash or share options
b. Zero-sum game
c. General purpose technologies
d. Gordon growth model

5. In game theory, a _____ is a game where one player chooses his action before the others choose theirs. Importantly, the later players must have some information of the first's choice, otherwise the difference in time would have no strategic effect. Extensive form representations are usually used for _____s, since they explicitly illustrate the sequential aspects of a game.

a. Comparative economic systems
b. Normative economics
c. Conglomerate merger
d. Sequential game

6. In game theory, _____ is a solution concept of a game involving two or more players, in which each player is assumed to know the equilibrium strategies of the other players, and no player has anything to gain by changing only his or her own strategy unilaterally. If each player has chosen a strategy and no player can benefit by changing his or her strategy while the other players keep theirs unchanged, then the current set of strategy choices and the corresponding payoffs constitute a _____.

Stated simply, Amy and Bill are in _____ if Amy is making the best decision she can, taking into account Bill's decision, and Bill is making the best decision he can, taking into account Amy's decision.

a. Proper equilibrium
b. Lump of labour
c. Linear production game
d. Nash equilibrium

7. The _____ is a trilateral trade bloc in North America created by the governments of the United States, Canada, and Mexico. The agreement creating the trade bloc came into force on January 1, 1994. It superseded the Canada-United States Free Trade Agreement between the U.S. and Canada.
   a. Case-Shiller Home Price Indices
   b. Federal Reserve Bank Notes
   c. Demand-side technologies
   d. North American Free Trade Agreement

8. The _____ is the apparent contradiction that although water is on the whole more useful, in terms of survival, than diamonds, diamonds command a higher price in the market. The economist Adam Smith is often considered to be the classic presenter of this paradox. Nicolaus Copernicus, John Locke, John Law and others had previously tried to explain the disparity.
   a. 100-year flood
   b. 130-30 fund
   c. Paradox of value
   d. St. Petersburg paradox

9. In game theory, a _____ is an extensive form game which consists in some number of repetitions of some base game (called a stage game.) The stage game is usually one of the well-studied 2-person games. It captures the idea that a player will have to take into account the impact of his current action on the future actions of other players; this is sometimes called his reputation.
   a. Quasi-perfect equilibrium
   b. Correlated equilibrium
   c. Pursuit-evasion
   d. Repeated game

10. _____ refers to methods in probability and statistics named after the Reverend Thomas Bayes (ca. 1702-1761), in particular methods related to:

   - the degree-of-belief interpretation of probability, as opposed to frequency or proportion or propensity interpretations; or
   - Bayes' theorem on conditional probability.

These methods include:

- Bayes estimator
- Bayes factor
- _____ average
- _____ spam filtering
- _____ game
- _____ inference
- _____ information criterion
- _____ multivariate linear regression
  - _____ linear regression, a special case
- _____ model comparison
- _____ network
- _____ probability
- Empirical Bayes method
- Naive Bayes classifier

_____ also refers to the application of this probability theory to the functioning of the brain

- _____ brain

a. Freedom Park
b. Fiscal
c. Technocracy
d. Bayesian

11. _____ in economics and business is the result of an exchange and from that trade we assign a numerical monetary value to a good, service or asset. If Alice trades Bob 4 apples for an orange, the _____ of an orange is 4 apples. Inversely, the _____ of an apple is 1/4 oranges.
   a. Price book
   b. Premium pricing
   c. Price
   d. Price war

12. In combinatorial game theory, a _____ is a directed graph whose nodes are positions in a game and whose edges are moves. The complete _____ for a game is the _____ starting at the initial position and containing all possible moves from each position. The first two ply of the _____ for tic-tac-toe.

The diagram shows the first two levels, or ply, in the _____ for tic-tac-toe.

a. Game complexity
b. Fuzzy game
c. Game tree
d. Map-coloring games

13. _____ is the advantage gained by the initial occupant of a market segment. This advantage may stem from the fact that the first entrant can gain control of resources that followers may not be able to match. Sometimes the first mover is not able to capitalise on its advantage, leaving the opportunity for another firm to gain second-mover advantage.
   a. First-mover advantage
   b. Business engineering
   c. Continuous Improvement Process
   d. Cross-docking

14. _____ is a fee paid on borrowed assets. It is the price paid for the use of borrowed money , or, money earned by deposited funds . Assets that are sometimes lent with _____ include money, shares, consumer goods through hire purchase, major assets such as aircraft, and even entire factories in finance lease arrangements.
   a. Asset protection
   b. Interest
   c. Internal debt
   d. Insolvency

15. A non-_____ is a term used in game theory economics to describe a threat by a player known to be rational in a sequential game that he would not carry out as it would not be in his best interest to do so. In game theoretical analysis the threat does not need to be a literally outspoken.

A simple example could be given by a person A walking up to another person B with a bomb.

   a. Credible threat
   b. Black-Scholes
   c. Debt to Assets
   d. Commodity fetishism

16. _____ refers to the objective and subjective components of the believability of a source or message.

Traditionally, _____ has two key components: trustworthiness and expertise, which both have objective and subjective components. Trustworthiness is a based more on subjective factors, but can include objective measurements such as established reliability.

a. 100-year flood
b. 130-30 fund
c. Credibility
d. 1921 recession

17. In business and accounting, _____ are everything of value that is owned by a person or company. It is a claim on the property your income of a borrower. The balance sheet of a firm records the monetary value of the _____ owned by the firm.
   a. ACCRA Cost of Living Index
   b. Assets
   c. Amortization schedule
   d. ACEA agreement

18. A natural resource is a _____ resource if it is replaced by natural processes at a rate comparable or faster than its rate of consumption by humans. Solar radiation, tides, winds and hydroelectricity are perpetual resources that are in no danger of long-term availability. _____ resources may also mean commodities such as wood, paper, and leather, if harvesting is performed in a sustainable manner.
   a. 130-30 fund
   b. 100-year flood
   c. Renewable
   d. 1921 recession

19. _____ is one of the constituents of a leasing calculus or operation. It describes the future value of a good in terms of percentage of depreciation of its initial value.
   a. Net pay
   b. Seasonal industry
   c. Real net output ratio
   d. Residual value

20. _____ is the a method of technical and economic research of the systems for purpose to optimize a parity between system's consumer functions or properties and expenses to achieve those functions or properties.

This methodology for continuous perfection of production, industrial technologies, organizational structures was developed by Juryj Sobolev in 1948 at the 'Perm telephone factory'

- 1948 Juryj Sobolev - the first success in application of a method analysis at the 'Perm telephone factory' .
- 1949 - the first application for the invention as result of use of the new method.

Chapter 13. Best-Practice Tactics: Game Theory

Today in economically developed countries practically each enterprise or the company use methodology of the kind of functional-cost analysis as a practice of the quality management, most full satisfying to principles of standards of series ISO 9000.

- Interest of consumer not in products itself, but the advantage which it will receive from its usage.
- The consumer aspires to reduce his expenses
- Functions needed by consumer can be executed in the various ways, and, hence, with various efficiency and expenses. Among possible alternatives of realization of functions exist such in which the parity of quality and the price is the optimal for the consumer.

The goal of _____ is achievement of the highest consumer satisfaction of production at simultaneous decrease in all kinds of industrial expenses Classical _____ has three English synonyms - Value Engineering, Value Management, Value Analysis.

a. Monopoly wage
b. Function cost analysis
c. Staple financing
d. Willingness to pay

Chapter 13. Best-Practice Tactics: Game Theory

21. A _____ is:

- Rewrite _____, in generative grammar and computer science
- Standardization, a formal and widely-accepted statement, fact, definition, or qualification
- Operation, a determinate _____ for performing a mathematical operation and obtaining a certain result (Mathematics, Logic)
    - Unary operation
    - Binary operation
- _____ of inference, a function from sets of formulae to formulae (Mathematics, Logic)
- _____ of thumb, principle with broad application that is not intended to be strictly accurate or reliable for every situation. Also often simply referred to as a _____
- Moral, an atomic element of a moral code for guiding choices in human behavior
- Heuristic, a quantized '_____' which shows a tendency or probability for successful function
- A regulation, as in sports
- A Production _____, as in computer science
- Procedural law, a _____ set governing the application of laws to cases
    - A law, which may informally be called a '_____'
    - A court ruling, a decision by a court
- In the U.S. Government, a regulation mandated by Congress, but written or expanded upon by the Executive Branch.
- Norm (sociology), an informal but widely accepted _____, concept, truth, definition, or qualification (social norms, legal norms, coding norms)
- Norm (philosophy), a kind of sentence or a reason to act, feel or believe
- 'Rulership' is the concept of governance by a government:
    - Military _____, governance by a military body
    - Monastic _____, a collection of precepts that guides the life of monks or nuns in a religious order where the superior holds the place of Christ
- Slide _____

- '_____,' a song by Ayumi Hamasaki
- '_____,' a song by rapper Nas
- '_____s,' an album by the band The Whitest Boy Alive
- _____s: Pyaar Ka Superhit Formula, a 2003 Bollywood film
- ruler, an instrument for measuring lengths
- _____, a component of an astrolabe, circumferator or similar instrument
- The _____s, a bestselling self-help book
- _____ Project (Run Up-to-date Linux Everywhere), a project that aims to use up-to-date Linux software on old PCs
- _____ engine, a software system that helps managing business _____s
- Ja _____, a hip hop artist
    - R.U.L.E., a 2005 greatest hits album by rapper Ja _____
- '_____s,' a KMFDM song

a. Technocracy
b. Procter ' Gamble
c. Rule
d. Demand

22. _____ is a concept with somewhat disparate meanings in several fields. It also has a common meaning which has a loose connection with some of those more definite meanings.

Casually, it is typically used to denote a lack of order, or purpose, or cause.

a. 1921 recession
b. Randomness
c. 100-year flood
d. 130-30 fund

23. _____ is the controlled distribution of resources and scarce goods or services. _____ controls the size of the ration, one's allotted portion of the resources being distributed on a particular day or at a particular time.

In economics, it is often common to use the word '_____' to refer to one of the roles that prices play in markets, while _____ is called 'non-price _____.' Using prices to ration means that those with the most money (or other assets) and who want a product the most are first to receive it.

a. Rationing
b. 1921 recession
c. 130-30 fund
d. 100-year flood

24. In economics, a _____ is a market served by only one firm, but with mandated 'competitive' pricing, so as to second the monopoly held by said firm on said market. Its fundamental feature is low barriers to entry and exit; a perfectly _____ would have no barriers to entry or exit. _____s are characteristed by 'hit and run' entry.

a. Market mechanism
b. Perfect market
c. Horizontal market
d. Contestable market

Chapter 14. Pricing Techniques and Analysis

1. _____ is one of the four Ps of the marketing mix. The other three aspects are product, promotion, and place. It is also a key variable in microeconomic price allocation theory.
   a. Pricing
   b. Point of total assumption
   c. Guaranteed Maximum Price
   d. Premium pricing

2. _____ was a writer, management consultant, and self-described 'social ecologist.' Widely considered to be 'the father of modern management,' his 39 books and countless scholarly and popular articles explored how humans are organized across all sectors of society--in business, government and the nonprofit world. His writings have predicted many of the major developments of the late twentieth century, including privatization and decentralization; the rise of Japan to economic world power; the decisive importance of marketing; and the emergence of the information society with its necessity of lifelong learning. In 1959, Drucker coined the term 'knowledge worker' and later in his life considered knowledge work productivity to be the next frontier of management.
   a. Thomas Mun
   b. George Cabot Lodge II
   c. Werner Sombart
   d. Peter Ferdinand Drucker

3. _____ in economics and business is the result of an exchange and from that trade we assign a numerical monetary value to a good, service or asset. If Alice trades Bob 4 apples for an orange, the _____ of an orange is 4 apples. Inversely, the _____ of an apple is 1/4 oranges.
   a. Price war
   b. Premium pricing
   c. Price book
   d. Price

4. A _____ is a hypothetical measure of overall prices for some set of goods and services, in a given region during a given interval, normalized relative to some base set. Typically, a _____ is approximated with a price index.

The classical dichotomy is the assumption that there is a relatively clean distinction between overall increases or decreases in prices and underlying, e;reale; economic variables.

   a. Discouraged worker
   b. Discretionary spending
   c. Price level
   d. Price elasticity of supply

Chapter 14. Pricing Techniques and Analysis

5. _____ is defined as the measure of responsiveness in the quantity demanded for a commodity as a result of change in price of the same commodity. It is a measure of how consumers react to a change in price. In other words, it is percentage change in quantity demanded as per the percentage change in price of the same commodity.
   a. 100-year flood
   b. 130-30 fund
   c. Price elasticity of demand
   d. 1921 recession

6. Economics:
   - _____, the desire to own something and the ability to pay for it
   - _____ curve, a graphic representation of a _____ schedule
   - _____ deposit, the money in checking accounts
   - _____ pull theory, the theory that inflation occurs when _____ for goods and services exceeds existing supplies
   - _____ schedule, a table that lists the quantity of a good a person will buy it each different price
   - _____ side economics, the school of economics at believes government spending and tax cuts open economy by raising _____

   a. McKesson ' Robbins scandal
   b. Production
   c. Demand
   d. Variability

7. In economics, _____ is the ratio of the percent change in one variable to the percent change in another variable. It is a tool for measuring the responsiveness of a function to changes in parameters in a relative way. Commonly analyzed are _____ of substitution, price and wealth.
   a. ACCRA Cost of Living Index
   b. ACEA agreement
   c. Elasticity of demand
   d. Elasticity

8. Price _____ is defined as the measure of responsiveness in the quantity demanded for a commodity as a result of change in price of the same commodity. It is a measure of how consumers react to a change in price. In other words, it is percentage change in quantity demanded by the percentage change in price of the same commodity.

a. Elasticity
b. Elasticity of demand
c. ACEA agreement
d. ACCRA Cost of Living Index

9. _____ or congestion charges is a system of surcharging users of a transport network in periods of peak demand to reduce traffic congestion. Examples include some toll-like road pricing fees, and higher peak charges for utilities, public transport and slots in canals and airports. This variable pricing strategy regulates demand, making it possible to manage congestion without increasing supply.
   a. 130-30 fund
   b. Congestion pricing
   c. 1921 recession
   d. 100-year flood

10. A _____ is a group of people or organizations sharing one or more characteristics that cause them to have similar product and/or service needs. A true _____ meets all of the following criteria: it is distinct from other segments (different segments have different needs), it is homogeneous within the segment (exhibits common needs); it responds similarly to a market stimulus, and it can be reached by a market intervention. The term is also used when consumers with identical product and/or service needs are divided up into groups so they can be charged different amounts.
    a. Pricing science
    b. Market Segmentation Index
    c. Customer to customer
    d. Market segment

11. A _____ is a duty imposed on goods when they are moved across a political boundary. They are usually associated with protectionism, the economic policy of restraining trade between nations. For political reasons, _____s are usually imposed on imported goods, although they may also be imposed on exported goods.
    a. Tariff
    b. 130-30 fund
    c. 100-year flood
    d. 1921 recession

12. A _____ is a price discrimination technique in which the price of a product or service is composed of two parts - a lump-sum fee as well as a per-unit charge. In general, price discrimination techniques only occur in partially or fully monopolistic markets. It is designed to enable the firm to capture more consumer surplus than it otherwise would in a non-discriminating pricing environment.

a. Price floor
b. Big ticket item
c. Penetration pricing
d. Two-part tariff

13. In microeconomics, the reservation (or reserve) price is the maximum price a buyer is willing to pay for a good or service; or, conversely, the minimum price at which a seller is willing to sell a good or service. _____s are commonly used in auctions.

_____s vary for the buyer according to their disposable income, their desire for the good, and the prices of, and their information about substitute goods.

a. Returns to scale
b. Mohring effect
c. Producer surplus
d. Reservation price

14. _____ exists when sales of identical goods or services are transacted at different prices from the same provider. In a theoretical market with perfect information, no transaction costs or prohibition on secondary exchange (or re-selling) to prevent arbitrage, _____ can only be a feature of monopoly and oligopoly markets, where market power can be exercised. Otherwise, the moment the seller tries to sell the same good at different prices, the buyer at the lower price can arbitrage by selling to the consumer buying at the higher price but with a tiny discount.

a. Price discrimination
b. Transfer pricing
c. Lerner Index
d. Loss leader

15. The _____ of 1936 (or Anti-Price Discrimination Act, 15 U.S.C. § 13) is a United States federal law that prohibits what were considered, at the time of passage, to be anticompetitive practices by producers, specifically price discrimination. It grew out of practices in which chain stores were allowed to purchase goods at lower prices than other retailers.

a. Contract theory
b. Flextime
c. Feoffee
d. Robinson-Patman Act

16. _____ Management is the succession of strategies used by management as a product goes through its _____. The conditions in which a product is sold changes over time and must be managed as it moves through its succession of stages.

The _____ goes through many phases, involves many professional disciplines, and requires many skills, tools and processes.

a. Tax profit
b. Procurement
c. Corporate tax
d. Product life cycle

17. _____ is a pricing strategy in which a marketer sets a relatively high price for a product or service at first, then lowers the price over time. It is a temporal version of price discrimination/yield management. It allows the firm to recover its sunk costs quickly before competition steps in and lowers the market price.

a. Price skimming
b. Price floor
c. Product sabotage
d. Two-part tariff

18. In cost-volume-profit analysis, a form of management accounting, _____ is the marginal profit per unit sale. It is a useful quantity in carrying out various calculations, and can be used as a measure of operating leverage.

The Total _____ is Total Revenue (TR, or Sales) minus Total Variable Cost (TVC):

TContribution margin = TR >− TVC

The Unit _____ (C) is Unit Revenue (Price, P) minus Unit Variable Cost (V):

C = P >− V

The _____ Ratio is the percentage of Contribution over Total Revenue, which can be calculated from the unit contribution over unit price or total contribution over Total Revenue:

For instance, if the price is $10 and the unit variable cost is $2, then the unit _____ is $8, and the _____ ratio is $8/$10 = 80%.

Chapter 14. Pricing Techniques and Analysis

a. Contribution margin
b. 100-year flood
c. 1921 recession
d. 130-30 fund

19. _____ is the process of understanding, anticipating and influencing consumer behavior in order to maximize revenue or profits from a fixed, perishable resource This process was first discovered by Dr. Matt H. Keller. The challenge is to sell the right resources to the right customer at the right time for the right price.
    a. Subscription
    b. Yield management
    c. Coopetition
    d. Freebie marketing

20.

_____ is, in very basic words, a position a firm occupies against its competitors.

According to Michael Porter, the three methods for creating a sustainable _____ are through:

1. Cost leadership - Cost advantage occurs when a firm delivers the same services as its competitors but at a lower cost;

2. Differentiation - Differentiation advantage occurs when a firm delivers greater services for the same price of its competitors. They are collectively known as positional advantages because they denote the firm's position in its industry as a leader in either superior services or cost;

3. Focus (economics) - A focused approach requires the firm to concentrate on a narrow, exclusive competitive segment (market niche), hoping to achieve a local rather than industry wide _____. There are cost focus seekers, who aim to obtain a local cost advantage over competition and differentiation focuser, who are looking for a local difference.

   a. National Diamond
   b. Chaos theory in organizational development
   c. Six Forces Model
   d. Competitive advantage

21. _____ is a term used to describe the sale of access to a service which exceeds the capacity of the service.

In the telecommunications industry, _____ -- such as in the frame relay world -- means that a telephone company has sold access to too many customers which basically flood the telephone company's lines, resulting in an inability for some customers to use what they purchased.

Nevertheless this only happens when all users try to use the service at the same time and since nearly half of the users will not use the service at the same moment this almost never happens.

   a. AD-IA Model
   b. ACEA agreement
   c. Overbooking
   d. ACCRA Cost of Living Index

Chapter 15. Contracting, Governance, and Organizational Form

1. _____ relates to decisions that define expectations, grant power, or verify performance. It consists either of a separate process or of a specific part of management or leadership processes. Sometimes people set up a government to administer these processes and systems.
   a. Governance
   b. 1921 recession
   c. 100-year flood
   d. 130-30 fund

2. The _____ or cash market is a commodities or securities market in which goods are sold for cash and delivered immediately. Contracts bought and sold on these markets are immediately effective. _____ s can operate wherever the infrastructure exists to conduct the transaction.
   a. Foreign exchange trading
   b. Triangular arbitrage
   c. Currency band
   d. Spot market

3. _____ is the prospect that a party insulated from risk may behave differently from the way it would behave if it were fully exposed to the risk. In insurance, _____ that occurs without conscious or malicious action is called morale hazard.

   _____ is related to information asymmetry, a situation in which one party in a transaction has more information than another.

   a. 1921 recession
   b. 100-year flood
   c. Moral hazard
   d. 130-30 fund

4. In political science and economics, the _____ or agency dilemma treats the difficulties that arise under conditions of incomplete and asymmetric information when a principal hires an agent, such as the problem that the two may not have the same interests, while the principal is, presumably, hiring the agent to pursue the interests of the former.

Various mechanisms may be used to try to align the interests of the agent with those of the principal, such as piece rates/commissions, profit sharing, efficiency wages, performance measurement (including financial statements), the agent posting a bond, or fear of firing. The _____ is found in most employer/employee relationships, for example, when stockholders hire top executives of corporations.

a. 100-year flood
b. Principal-agent problem
c. 1921 recession
d. 130-30 fund

5. In economics and sociology, an _____ is any factor (financial or non-financial) that enables or motivates a particular course of action, or counts as a reason for preferring one choice to the alternatives. It is an expectation that encourages people to behave in a certain way. Since human beings are purposeful creatures, the study of _____ structures is central to the study of all economic activity (both in terms of individual decision-making and in terms of co-operation and competition within a larger institutional structure.)
   a. Economic reform
   b. Epstein-Zin preferences
   c. Isocost
   d. Incentive

6. In mechanism design, a process is said to be incentive compatible if all of the participants fare best when they truthfully reveal any private information asked for by the mechanism . As an illustration, voting systems which create incentives to vote dishonestly lack the property of _____. In the absence of dummy bidders or collusion, a second price auction is an example of mechanism that is incentive compatible.
   a. ACCRA Cost of Living Index
   b. AD-IA Model
   c. Incentive compatibility
   d. ACEA agreement

7. In business and accounting, _____ are everything of value that is owned by a person or company. It is a claim on the property your income of a borrower. The balance sheet of a firm records the monetary value of the _____ owned by the firm.
   a. Amortization schedule
   b. ACEA agreement
   c. ACCRA Cost of Living Index
   d. Assets

8. _____ is a theory that describes decisions between alternatives that involve risk, i.e. alternatives with uncertain outcomes, where the probabilities are known. The model is descriptive: it tries to model real-life choices, rather than optimal decisions.

_____ was developed by Daniel Kahneman, professor at Princeton University's Department of Psychology, and Amos Tversky in 1979 as a psychologically realistic alternative to expected utility theory.

Chapter 15. Contracting, Governance, and Organizational Form 101

a. Keynesian beauty contest
b. Mental accounting
c. Loss aversion
d. Prospect theory

9. A _____ is an entity formed between two or more parties to undertake economic activity together. The parties agree to create a new entity by both contributing equity, and they then share in the revenues, expenses, and control of the enterprise. The venture can be for one specific project only, or a continuing business relationship such as the Fuji Xerox _____.
   a. Joint venture
   b. Nexus of contracts
   c. Business valuation
   d. Property right

10. An _____ is a person who has possession of an enterprise and assumes significant accountability for the inherent risks and the outcome. It is an ambitious leader who combines land, labor, and capital to create and market new goods or services. The term is a loanword from French and was first defined by the Irish economist Richard Cantillon.
    a. Expansionary policies
    b. ACEA agreement
    c. ACCRA Cost of Living Index
    d. Entrepreneur

11. In economics and game theory, _____ is the study of designing rules of a game or system to achieve a specific outcome, even though each agent may be self-interested. This is done by setting up a structure in which agents have an incentive to behave according to the rules. The resulting mechanism is then said to implement the desired outcome.
    a. Mechanism design
    b. Fictitious play
    c. Proper equilibrium
    d. No-win situation

12. A _____ is a type of business entity in which partners (owners) share with each other the profits or losses of the business _____s are often favored over corporations for taxation purposes, as the _____ structure does not generally incur a tax on profits before it is distributed to the partners (i.e. there is no dividend tax levied.) However, depending on the _____ structure and the jurisdiction in which it operates, owners of a _____ may be exposed to greater personal liability than they would as shareholders of a corporation.

    For a country-by-country listing of types of _____s, companies, etc., see Types of business entity.

a. Partnership
b. Feoffee
c. Due diligence
d. Minimum wage law

13. _____s is the social science that studies the production, distribution, and consumption of goods and services. The term _____s comes from the Ancient Greek oá¼°κονομῖα from oá¼¶κος (oikos, 'house') + vÏŒμος (nomos, 'custom' or 'law'), hence 'rules of the house(hold)'. Current _____ models developed out of the broader field of political economy in the late 19th century, owing to a desire to use an empirical approach more akin to the physical sciences.
    a. Energy economics
    b. Opportunity cost
    c. Inflation
    d. Economic

14. _____ is the process of making predictions about the economy as a whole or in part.

Relevant models include

- Economic base analysis
- Shift-share analysis
- Input-output model
- Grinold and Kroner Model

   a. Economic forecasting
   b. Australian Financial Services Licence
   c. Overproduction
   d. Investment goods

15. _____ is the process of estimation in unknown situations. Prediction is a similar, but more general term. Both can refer to estimation of time series, cross-sectional or longitudinal data.
    a. 130-30 fund
    b. 100-year flood
    c. 1921 recession
    d. Forecasting

16. _____ or the economics of information is a branch of microeconomic theory that studies how information affects an economy and economic decisions. Information has special characteristics. It is easy to create but hard to trust.

a. AD-IA Model
b. ACCRA Cost of Living Index
c. ACEA agreement
d. Information economics

Chapter 15. Contracting, Governance, and Organizational Form

17. A _____ is:

   - Rewrite _____, in generative grammar and computer science
   - Standardization, a formal and widely-accepted statement, fact, definition, or qualification
   - Operation, a determinate _____ for performing a mathematical operation and obtaining a certain result (Mathematics, Logic)
     - Unary operation
     - Binary operation
   - _____ of inference, a function from sets of formulae to formulae (Mathematics, Logic)
   - _____ of thumb, principle with broad application that is not intended to be strictly accurate or reliable for every situation. Also often simply referred to as a _____
   - Moral, an atomic element of a moral code for guiding choices in human behavior
   - Heuristic, a quantized '_____' which shows a tendency or probability for successful function
   - A regulation, as in sports
   - A Production _____, as in computer science
   - Procedural law, a _____ set governing the application of laws to cases
     - A law, which may informally be called a '_____'
     - A court ruling, a decision by a court
   - In the U.S. Government, a regulation mandated by Congress, but written or expanded upon by the Executive Branch.
   - Norm (sociology), an informal but widely accepted _____, concept, truth, definition, or qualification (social norms, legal norms, coding norms)
   - Norm (philosophy), a kind of sentence or a reason to act, feel or believe
   - 'Rulership' is the concept of governance by a government:
     - Military _____, governance by a military body
     - Monastic _____, a collection of precepts that guides the life of monks or nuns in a religious order where the superior holds the place of Christ
   - Slide _____

   - '_____,' a song by Ayumi Hamasaki
   - '_____,' a song by rapper Nas
   - '_____s,' an album by the band The Whitest Boy Alive
   - _____s: Pyaar Ka Superhit Formula, a 2003 Bollywood film
   - ruler, an instrument for measuring lengths
   - _____, a component of an astrolabe, circumferator or similar instrument
   - The _____s, a bestselling self-help book
   - _____ Project (Run Up-to-date Linux Everywhere), a project that aims to use up-to-date Linux software on old PCs
   - _____ engine, a software system that helps managing business _____s
   - Ja _____, a hip hop artist
     - R.U.L.E., a 2005 greatest hits album by rapper Ja _____
   - '_____s,' a KMFDM song

Chapter 15. Contracting, Governance, and Organizational Form   105

a. Technocracy
b. Demand
c. Procter ' Gamble
d. Rule

18. _____ is a service policy where by the requests of customers or clients are attended to in the order that they arrived, without other biases or preferences. The policy can be employed when processing sales orders, in determining restaurant seating, or on a taxi stand, for example.

Festival seating (also known as general seating and stadium seating) is seating done on a FCFS basis.

a. 130-30 fund
b. 100-year flood
c. 1921 recession
d. First-come, first-served

19. A _____ is a type of auction where the auctioneer begins with a high asking price which is lowered until some participant is willing to accept the auctioneer's price, or a predetermined reserve price (the seller's minimum acceptable price) is reached. The winning participant pays the last announced price. This is also known as a 'clock auction' or an open-outcry descending-price auction.

a. Vickrey auction
b. Dutch auction
c. Box social
d. French auction

20. An _____ is a type of auction, whose most typical form is the 'open outcry' auction. The auctioneer opens the auction by announcing a Suggested Opening Bid, a starting price or reserve for the item on sale and then accepts increasingly higher bids from the floor consisting of buyers with a possible interest in the item. Unlike sealed bid auctions, 'open outcry' auctions are 'open' or fully transparent as the identity of all bidders is disclosed to each other bidder during the auction.

a. Auction school
b. Online auction business model
c. Auction sniping
d. English auction

21. _____ is an offer (often competitive) of setting a price one is willing to pay for something. A price offer is called a bid. The term may be used in context of auctions, stock exchange, card games, or real estate transactions.

a. Normal good
b. Bord halfpenny
c. Central limit order book
d. Bidding

22. _____ refers to methods in probability and statistics named after the Reverend Thomas Bayes (ca. 1702-1761), in particular methods related to:

- the degree-of-belief interpretation of probability, as opposed to frequency or proportion or propensity interpretations; or
- Bayes' theorem on conditional probability.

These methods include:

- Bayes estimator
- Bayes factor
- _____ average
- _____ spam filtering
- _____ game
- _____ inference
- _____ information criterion
- _____ multivariate linear regression
    - _____ linear regression, a special case
- _____ model comparison
- _____ network
- _____ probability
- Empirical Bayes method
- Naive Bayes classifier

_____ also refers to the application of this probability theory to the functioning of the brain

- _____ brain

a. Fiscal
b. Technocracy
c. Freedom Park
d. Bayesian

Chapter 15. Contracting, Governance, and Organizational Form

23. _____ is a concept in economics, finance, and psychology related to the behaviour of consumers and investors under uncertainty. _____ is the reluctance of a person to accept a bargain with an uncertain payoff rather than another bargain with a more certain, but possibly lower, expected payoff. For example, a risk-averse investor might choose to put his or her money into a bank account with a low but guaranteed interest rate, rather than into a stock that is likely to have high returns, but also has a chance of becoming worthless.

   a. Compound annual growth rate
   b. Reinsurance
   c. Risk theory
   d. Risk aversion

24. A _____ is the transfer of wealth from one party (such as a person or company) to another. A _____ is usually made in exchange for the provision of goods, services or both, or to fulfill a legal obligation.

   The simplest and oldest form of _____ is barter, the exchange of one good or service for another.

   a. Soft count
   b. Social gravity
   c. Going concern
   d. Payment

25. _____ is defined as excess of actual cost over budget. _____ is also sometimes called 'cost escalation,' 'cost increase,' or 'budget overrun.' However, cost escalation and increases do not necessarily result in _____ s if cost escalation is included in the budget.

   _____ is common in infrastructure, building, and technology projects.

   a. Sliding scale fees
   b. Marginal cost
   c. Khozraschyot
   d. Cost overrun

Chapter 16. Government Regulation

1. In law and economics, the _____, describes the economic efficiency of an economic allocation or outcome in the presence of externalities. The theorem states that when trade in an externality is possible and there are no transaction costs, bargaining will lead to an efficient outcome regardless of the initial allocation of property rights. In practice, obstacles to bargaining or poorly defined property rights can prevent Coasian bargaining.
   a. General Mining Act of 1872
   b. Means test
   c. Prior appropriation water rights
   d. Coase Theorem

2. _____ is the removal or simplification of government rules and regulations that constrain the operation of market forces. _____ does not mean elimination of laws against fraud, but eliminating or reducing government control of how business is done, thereby moving toward a more free market.

The stated rationale for '_____' is often that fewer and simpler regulations will lead to a raised level of competitiveness, therefore higher productivity, more efficiency and lower prices overall.

   a. Deregulation
   b. Macroeconomic policy instruments
   c. Secular basis
   d. Fundamental psychological law

3. In economics, _____ describes the state of a market with respect to competition.

   - Perfect competition, in which the market consists of a very large number of firms producing a homogeneous product.
   - Monopolistic competition where there are a large number of independent firms which have a very small proportion of the market share.
   - Oligopoly, in which a market is dominated by a small number of firms which own more than 40% of the market share.
   - Oligopsony, a market dominated by many sellers and a few buyers.
   - Monopoly, where there is only one provider of a product or service.
   - Natural monopoly, a monopoly in which economies of scale cause efficiency to increase continuously with the size of the firm. A firm is a natural monopoly if it is able to serve the entire market demand at a lower cost than any combination of two or more smaller, more specialized firms.
   - Monopsony, when there is only one buyer in a market.

The imperfectly competitive structure is quite identical to the realistic market conditions where some monopolistic competitors, monopolists, oligopolists, and duopolists exist and dominate the market conditions. The elements of _____ include the number and size distribution of firms, entry conditions, and the extent of differentiation.

These somewhat abstract concerns tend to determine some but not all details of a specific concrete market system where buyers and sellers actually meet and commit to trade.

Chapter 16. Government Regulation

   a. Monopolistic competition
   b. Human capital
   c. Labour economics
   d. Market structure

4. In economics and especially in the theory of competition, _____ are obstacles in the path of a firm that make it difficult to enter a given market.

_____ are the source of a firm's pricing power - the ability of a firm to raise prices without losing all its customers.

The term refers to hindrances that an individual may face while trying to gain entrance into a profession or trade.

   a. Social dumping
   b. Limit price
   c. Group boycott
   d. Barriers to entry

5. _____ in economics and business is the result of an exchange and from that trade we assign a numerical monetary value to a good, service or asset. If Alice trades Bob 4 apples for an orange, the _____ of an orange is 4 apples. Inversely, the _____ of an apple is 1/4 oranges.
   a. Price book
   b. Price
   c. Price war
   d. Premium pricing

6. Competition law, known in the United States as _____ law, has three main elements:

   - prohibiting agreements or practices that restrict free trading and competition between business entities. This includes in particular the repression of cartels.
   - banning abusive behaviour by a firm dominating a market, or anti-competitive practices that tend to lead to such a dominant position. Practices controlled in this way may include predatory pricing, tying, price gouging, refusal to deal, and many others.
   - supervising the mergers and acquisitions of large corporations, including some joint ventures. Transactions that are considered to threaten the competitive process can be prohibited altogether, or approved subject to 'remedies' such as an obligation to divest part of the merged business or to offer licences or access to facilities to enable other businesses to continue competing.

The substance and practice of competition law varies from jurisdiction to jurisdiction. Protecting the interests of consumers (consumer welfare) and ensuring that entrepreneurs have an opportunity to compete in the market economy are often treated as important objectives. Competition law is closely connected with law on deregulation of access to markets, state aids and subsidies, the privatisation of state owned assets and the establishment of independent sector regulators. In recent decades, competition law has been viewed as a way to provide better public services.

a. Intellectual property law
b. Antitrust
c. Anti-Inflation Act
d. United Kingdom competition law

7. The _____ is an independent agency of the United States government, established in 1914 by the _____ Act. Its principal mission is the promotion of 'consumer protection' and the elimination and prevention of what regulators perceive to be harmfully 'anti-competitive' business practices, such as coercive monopoly.

The _____ Act was one of President Wilson's major acts against trusts.

a. 1921 recession
b. 100-year flood
c. Federal Trade Commission
d. 130-30 fund

8. The _____ of 1914 (15 U.S.C §§ 41-58, as amended) established the Federal Trade Commission (FTC), a bipartisan body of five members appointed by the President of the United States for seven year terms. This Commission was authorized to issue Cease and Desist orders to large corporations to curb unfair trade practices. This Act also gave more flexibility to the US congress for judicial matters.
a. Federal Trade Commission Act
b. Buydown
c. Minimum wage law
d. Competition law theory

9. The _____ of 1936 (or Anti-Price Discrimination Act, 15 U.S.C. § 13) is a United States federal law that prohibits what were considered, at the time of passage, to be anticompetitive practices by producers, specifically price discrimination. It grew out of practices in which chain stores were allowed to purchase goods at lower prices than other retailers.

a. Contract theory
b. Feoffee
c. Flextime
d. Robinson-Patman Act

10. _____ is an agreement between business competitors to sell the same product or service at the same price. In general, it is an agreement intended to ultimately push the price of a product as high as possible, leading to profits for all the sellers. Price-fixing can also involve any agreement to fix, peg, discount or stabilize prices.

a. Non-price competition
b. Moral victory
c. Cut-throat competition
d. Price fixing

11. In economics, _____ is a function of the number of firms and their respective shares of the total production (alternatively, total capacity or total reserves) in a market. Alternative terms are Industry concentration and Seller concentration.

_____ is related to the concept of industrial concentration, which concerns the distribution of production within an industry, as opposed to a market.

a. Decartelization
b. Market concentration
c. Quasi-rent
d. Monopolization

12. The phrase _____ and acquisitions refers to the aspect of corporate strategy, corporate finance and management dealing with the buying, selling and combining of different companies that can aid, finance, or help a growing company in a given industry grow rapidly without having to create another business entity.

An acquisition, also known as a takeover or a buyout, is the buying of one company (the 'target') by another. An acquisition may be friendly or hostile.

a. Differential accumulation
b. Mergers
c. Political economy
d. Peace dividend

13. In economics, the _____ of an industry is used as an indicator of the relative size of firms in relation to the industry as a whole. It is calculated as the sum of the percent market share of the top n industries. This may also assist in determining the market structure of the industry.

 a. Concentration ratio
 b. Pacman conjecture
 c. Quasi-rent
 d. Monopolization

14. A _____ is an expression that compares quantities relative to each other. The most common examples involve two quantities, but any number of quantities can be compared. _____s are represented mathematically by separating each quantity with a colon, for example the _____ 2:3, which is read as the _____ 'two to three'.

 a. 130-30 fund
 b. 100-year flood
 c. Y-intercept
 d. Ratio

15. The _____ are a set of internal rules promulgated by the Antitrust Division of the United States Department of Justice (DOJ) in conjunction with the Federal Trade Commission (FTC.) These rules, which have been revised a number of times in the past four decades, govern the extent to which these two regulatory bodies will scrutinize and/or challenge a potential merger on grounds of market concentration or threat to competition within a relevant market.

The _____ have sections governing both horizontal integration and vertical integration.

 a. No-FEAR Act
 b. Law of increasing relative cost
 c. Merger guidelines
 d. Business valuation

16. The term _____ refers to an offense under Section 2 of the American Sherman Antitrust Act, passed in 1890. Section 2 states that any person 'who shall monopolize .

 a. Bilateral monopoly
 b. Quasi-rent
 c. Complementary monopoly
 d. Monopolization

17. _____ exists when sales of identical goods or services are transacted at different prices from the same provider. In a theoretical market with perfect information, no transaction costs or prohibition on secondary exchange (or re-selling) to prevent arbitrage, _____ can only be a feature of monopoly and oligopoly markets, where market power can be exercised. Otherwise, the moment the seller tries to sell the same good at different prices, the buyer at the lower price can arbitrage by selling to the consumer buying at the higher price but with a tiny discount.

  a. Transfer pricing
  b. Loss leader
  c. Lerner Index
  d. Price discrimination

18. _____ is one of several anti-competitive practices forbidden in countries which have restricted market economies. For example, in Australia:

- Agreements involving competitors that involve restricting the supply of goods are prohibited if they have the purpose or effect of substantially lessening competition in a market in which the businesses operate.

'_____' Reference: The Competition Act, 2002 (India) S4-d.'_____' includes any agreement which restricts, or is likely to restrict, by any method the persons or classes of persons to whom goods are sold or from whom goods are bought

  a. Refusal to deal
  b. Poverty penalty
  c. Microcap stock
  d. Payment gateway

19. A _____ is an externality which operates through prices rather than through real resource effects. For example, an influx of city-dwellers buying second homes in a rural area can drive up house prices, making it difficult for young people in the area to get onto the property ladder.

This is in contrast with technical or real externalities which have a direct resource effect on a third party.

  a. Guaranteed Maximum Price
  b. Discounts and allowances
  c. Pricing
  d. Pecuniary externality

20. In economics, an _____ or spillover of an economic transaction is an impact on a party that is not directly involved in the transaction. In such a case, prices do not reflect the full costs or benefits in production or consumption of a product or service. A positive impact is called an external benefit, while a negative impact is called an external cost.

a. Externality
b. Existence value
c. Environmental impact assessment
d. Environmental tariff

21. To _____ is to impose a financial charge or other levy upon a taxpayer by a state or the functional equivalent of a state.

_____es are also imposed by many subnational entities. _____es consist of direct _____ or indirect _____, and may be paid in money or as its labour equivalent (often but not always unpaid.)

a. Tax
b. 1921 recession
c. 100-year flood
d. 130-30 fund

22. To tax is to impose a financial charge or other levy upon a taxpayer by a state or the functional equivalent of a state.

_____ are also imposed by many subnational entities. _____ consist of direct tax or indirect tax, and may be paid in money or as its labour equivalent (often but not always unpaid.)

a. 100-year flood
b. Taxes
c. 1921 recession
d. 130-30 fund

23. A _____ is a set of exclusive rights granted by a state to an inventor or his assignee for a limited period of time in exchange for a disclosure of an invention.

The procedure for granting _____s, the requirements placed on the _____ee and the extent of the exclusive rights vary widely between countries according to national laws and international agreements. Typically, however, a _____ application must include one or more claims defining the invention which must be new, inventive, and useful or industrially applicable.

a. Patent
b. Bank regulation
c. Bona fide occupational qualification
d. Long service leave

24. _____s is the social science that studies the production, distribution, and consumption of goods and services. The term _____s comes from the Ancient Greek oá¼°κονομῖα from oá¼¶κος (oikos, 'house') + vΐŒμος (nomos, 'custom' or 'law'), hence 'rules of the house(hold)'. Current _____ models developed out of the broader field of political economy in the late 19th century, owing to a desire to use an empirical approach more akin to the physical sciences.
   a. Energy economics
   b. Opportunity cost
   c. Inflation
   d. Economic

25. _____ is the process of making predictions about the economy as a whole or in part.

Relevant models include

- Economic base analysis
- Shift-share analysis
- Input-output model
- Grinold and Kroner Model

   a. Australian Financial Services Licence
   b. Investment goods
   c. Overproduction
   d. Economic forecasting

26. _____ is the process of estimation in unknown situations. Prediction is a similar, but more general term. Both can refer to estimation of time series, cross-sectional or longitudinal data.
   a. 1921 recession
   b. 130-30 fund
   c. 100-year flood
   d. Forecasting

Chapter 17. Long-Term Investment Analysis

1. In finance, valuation is the process of estimating the potential market value of a financial asset or liability. Valuations can be done on assets (for example, investments in marketable securities such as stocks, options, business enterprises, or intangible assets such as patents and trademarks) or on liabilities (e.g., Bonds issued by a company.) Valuations are required in many contexts including _____, capital budgeting, merger and acquisition transactions, financial reporting, taxable events to determine the proper tax liability, and in litigation.
    a. ACCRA Cost of Living Index
    b. ACEA agreement
    c. AD-IA Model
    d. Investment analysis

2. _____ was a U.S. hedge fund which used trading strategies such as fixed income arbitrage, statistical arbitrage, and pairs trading, combined with high leverage. It failed spectacularly in the late 1990s, leading to a massive bailout by other major banks and investment houses, which was supervised by the Federal Reserve.

    LTCM was founded in 1994 by John Meriwether, the former vice-chairman and head of bond trading at Salomon Brothers.

    a. General purpose technologies
    b. Consumer protection
    c. Long-term capital management
    d. Collectivization of agriculture in Romania

3. _____s (CAPEX or capex) are expenditures creating future benefits. A _____ is incurred when a business spends money either to buy fixed assets or to add to the value of an existing fixed asset with a useful life that extends beyond the taxable year. Capex are used by a company to acquire or upgrade physical assets such as equipment, property, or industrial buildings.
    a. Wealth inequality in the United States
    b. Cost of capital
    c. Modigliani-Miller theorem
    d. Capital expenditure

4. _____ is the planning process used to determine whether a firm's long term investments such as new machinery, replacement machinery, new plants, new products, and research development projects are worth pursuing. It is budget for major capital, or investment, expenditures.

Chapter 17. Long-Term Investment Analysis

Many formal methods are used in _____, including the techniques such as

- Net present value
- Profitability index
- Internal rate of return
- Modified Internal Rate of Return
- Equivalent annuity

These methods use the incremental cash flows from each potential investment, or project. Techniques based on accounting earnings and accounting rules are sometimes used - though economists consider this to be improper - such as the accounting rate of return, and 'return on investment.' Simplified and hybrid methods are used as well, such as payback period and discounted payback period.

a. Participating preferred stock
b. Voting interest
c. Preferred stock
d. Capital budgeting

5. _____ refers to the movement of cash into or out of a business or financial product. It is usually measured during a specified, finite period of time. Measurement of _____ can be used

- to determine a project's rate of return or value. The time of _____s into and out of projects are used as inputs in financial models such as internal rate of return, and net present value.
- to determine problems with a business's liquidity. Being profitable does not necessarily mean being liquid. A company can fail because of a shortage of cash, even while profitable.
- as an alternate measure of a business's profits when it is believed that accrual accounting concepts do not represent economic realities. For example, a company may be notionally profitable but generating little operational cash (as may be the case for a company that barters its products rather than selling for cash.) In such a case, the company may be deriving additional operating cash by issuing shares evaluating default risk, re-investment requirements, etc.

_____ is a generic term used differently depending on the context. It may be defined by users for their own purposes.

a. Strip financing
b. Restricted stock
c. Second lien loan
d. Cash flow

6. In finance, _____ rate of profit or sometimes just return, is the ratio of money gained or lost on an investment relative to the amount of money invested. The amount of money gained or lost may be referred to as interest, profit/loss, gain/loss, or net income/loss. The money invested may be referred to as the asset, capital, principal, or the cost basis of the investment.

  a. Rate of return
  b. Current ratio
  c. Sortino ratio
  d. Cost accrual ratio

7. _____ or net present worth (NPW) is defined as the total present value (PV) of a time series of cash flows. It is a standard method for using the time value of money to appraise long-term projects. Used for capital budgeting, and widely throughout economics, it measures the excess or shortfall of cash flows, in present value terms, once financing charges are met.

  a. Maturity
  b. Future value
  c. Net present value
  d. Refinancing risk

8. _____ is the value on a given date of a future payment or series of future payments, discounted to reflect the time value of money and other factors such as investment risk. _____ calculations are widely used in business and economics to provide a means to compare cash flows at different times on a meaningful 'like to like' basis.

Money value fluctuates over time: $100 today are not worth $100 in five years.

  a. Future value
  b. Tax shield
  c. Present value of costs
  d. Present value

9. _____ is the a method of technical and economic research of the systems for purpose to optimize a parity between system's consumer functions or properties and expenses to achieve those functions or properties.

This methodology for continuous perfection of production, industrial technologies, organizational structures was developed by Juryj Sobolev in 1948 at the 'Perm telephone factory'

- 1948 Juryj Sobolev - the first success in application of a method analysis at the 'Perm telephone factory'.
- 1949 - the first application for the invention as result of use of the new method.

Chapter 17. Long-Term Investment Analysis

Today in economically developed countries practically each enterprise or the company use methodology of the kind of functional-cost analysis as a practice of the quality management, most full satisfying to principles of standards of series ISO 9000.

- Interest of consumer not in products itself, but the advantage which it will receive from its usage.
- The consumer aspires to reduce his expenses
- Functions needed by consumer can be executed in the various ways, and, hence, with various efficiency and expenses. Among possible alternatives of realization of functions exist such in which the parity of quality and the price is the optimal for the consumer.

The goal of _____ is achievement of the highest consumer satisfaction of production at simultaneous decrease in all kinds of industrial expenses Classical _____ has three English synonyms - Value Engineering, Value Management, Value Analysis.

a. Function cost analysis
b. Staple financing
c. Willingness to pay
d. Monopoly wage

10. The _____ is an expected return that the provider of capital plans to earn on their investment.

Capital (money) used for funding a business should earn returns for the capital providers who risk their capital. For an investment to be worthwhile, the expected return on capital must be greater than the _____.

a. Capital expenditure
b. Modigliani-Miller theorem
c. Capital intensive
d. Cost of capital

11. _____ is that which is owed; usually referencing assets owed, but the term can also cover moral obligations and other interactions not requiring money. In the case of assets, _____ is a means of using future purchasing power in the present before a summation has been earned. Some companies and corporations use _____ as a part of their overall corporate finance strategy.

a. Hard money loan
b. Debenture
c. Collateral Management
d. Debt

12. _____ is the capital that a business raises by taking out a loan. It is a loan made to a company that is normally repaid at some future date. _____ differs from equity or share capital because subscribers to _____ do not become part owners of the business, but are merely creditors, and the suppliers of _____ usually receive a contractually fixed annual percentage return on their loan, and this is known as the coupon rate.

   a. Financial rand
   b. Debt cash flow
   c. Blank endorsement
   d. Debt capital

13. _____ are costs incurred on the purchase of land, buildings, construction and equipment to be used in the production of goods or the rendering of services. In other words, the total cost needed to bring a project to a commercially operable status. However, _____ are not limited to the initial construction of a factory or other business.

   a. Blanket order
   b. Total revenue
   c. Whitemail
   d. Capital costs

14. _____s are payments made by a corporation to its shareholders. It is the portion of corporate profits paid out to stockholders. When a corporation earns a profit or surplus, that money can be put to two uses: it can either be re-invested in the business (called retained earnings), or it can be paid to the shareholders as a _____.

   a. Dividend puzzle
   b. Dividend cover
   c. Dividend yield
   d. Dividend

15. _____ is the concept or idea of fairness in economics, particularly as to taxation or welfare economics.

In welfare economics, _____ may be distinguished from economic efficiency in overall evaluation of social welfare. Although '_____' has broader uses, it may be posed as a counterpart to economic inequality in yielding a 'good' distribution of welfare.

   a. ACCRA Cost of Living Index
   b. ACEA agreement
   c. AD-IA Model
   d. Equity

Chapter 17. Long-Term Investment Analysis

16. The term _____ has three unrelated technical definitions, and is also used in a variety of non-technical ways.

- In financial economics, it refers to any asset used to make money, as opposed to assets used for personal enjoyment or consumption. This is an important distinction because two people can disagree sharply about the value of personal assets, one person might think a sports car is more valuable than a pickup truck, another person might have the opposite taste. But if an asset is held for the purpose of making money, taste has nothing to do with it, only differences of opinion about how much money the asset will produce. With the further assumption that people agree on the probability distribution of future cash flows, it is possible to have an objective _____ pricing model. Even without the assumption of agreement, it is possible to set rational limits on _____ value.
- In governmental accounting, it is defined as any asset used in operations with an initial useful life extending beyond one reporting period. Generally, government managers have a 'stewardship' duty to maintain _____s under their control. See International Public Sector Accounting Standards for details.
- In US tax accounting, it is defined as any property other than a list of exceptions. The main exceptions are anything held for sale, and any real estate or depreciable property used in business. Almost everything you own and use for personal purposes, pleasure or investment is a _____. If something is a _____ for tax purposes, gains or losses on sale or disposition are capital gains or capital losses. For individuals, however, capital losses on property held for personal use are generally not deductible. See the IRS publication Tax Facts about Capital Gains and Losses for details.

A well-known financial accounting textbook advises that the term be avoided except in tax accounting because it is used in so many different senses, not all of them well-defined. For example it is often used as a synonym for fixed assets or for investments in securities.

A common non-technical usage occurs when people ask that employees or the environment or something else be treated as a _____.

a. Dynamic asset allocation
b. Capital asset
c. Consumption beta
d. Mid price

17. In business and accounting, _____ are everything of value that is owned by a person or company. It is a claim on the property your income of a borrower. The balance sheet of a firm records the monetary value of the _____ owned by the firm.
a. Amortization schedule
b. ACEA agreement
c. ACCRA Cost of Living Index
d. Assets

18. _____ is one of the four Ps of the marketing mix. The other three aspects are product, promotion, and place. It is also a key variable in microeconomic price allocation theory.

Chapter 17. Long-Term Investment Analysis

a. Pricing
b. Point of total assumption
c. Guaranteed Maximum Price
d. Premium pricing

19. _____ is the average weighted of cost of equity capital (ke) and cost of debt (kd.)

According to the 'Modigliani-Miller theorem', under certain assumptions a firm's WACC remains constant regardless of changes in its capital structure. These assumptions are outlined below:

1. Assume no individual or corporate taxes
2. Assume that individuals are able to borrow at the same rate as the firm, (known as home-made gearing)
3. Assume that the market is frictionless, that is no there are no transaction costs
4. Assume that the company has a fixed investment policy being implemented in the strategy of the company

Furthermore, M'M theory hypotheses that the cost of equity capital does change as the company increase its gearing level in the same direction of the gearing level. The reason is that as a company increases its leverage, the shareholders require a higher rate of return because the higher fixed interest costs lead to a higher variance in earnings.

a. Seemingly unrelated regression
b. Censored regression models
c. Weighted cost of capital
d. Method of simulated moments

20. _____ is a term that refers both to:

- a formal discipline used to help appraise, or assess, the case for a project or proposal, which itself is a process known as project appraisal; and
- an informal approach to making decisions of any kind.

Under both definitions the process involves, whether explicitly or implicitly, weighing the total expected costs against the total expected benefits of one or more actions in order to choose the best or most profitable option. The formal process is often referred to as either CBA (_____) or BCost-benefit analysis

Chapter 17. Long-Term Investment Analysis

A hallmark of CBA is that all benefits and all costs are expressed in money terms, and are adjusted for the time value of money, so that all flows of benefits and flows of project costs over time (which tend to occur at different points in time) are expressed on a common basis in terms of their e;present value.e; Closely related, but slightly different, formal techniques include Cost-effectiveness analysis, Economic impact analysis, Fiscal impact analysis and Social Return on Investment(SROI) analysis. The latter builds upon the logic of _____, but differs in that it is explicitly designed to inform the practical decision-making of enterprise managers and investors focused on optimising their social and environmental impacts.

a. 100-year flood
b. 130-30 fund
c. Decision theory
d. Cost-benefit analysis

21. _____ is a measure used to help guide choices about the value of diverting funds to social projects. It is defined as e;the appropriate value of r to use in computing present discount value for social investmentse; . A _____ is sometimes denoted as _____.

a. Reprivatization
b. Social discount rate
c. Privatization
d. Compound empowerment

22. Discounting is a financial mechanism in which a debtor obtains the right to delay payments to a creditor, for a defined period of time, in exchange for a charge or fee. Essentially, the party that owes money in the present purchases the right to delay the payment until some future date. The _____, or charge, is simply the difference between the original amount owed in the present and the amount that has to be paid in the future to settle the debt.

a. Certified Risk Manager
b. Reliability theory
c. Reinsurance
d. Discount

23. The _____ is an interest rate a central bank charges depository institutions that borrow reserves from it.

Chapter 17. Long-Term Investment Analysis

The term _____ has two meanings:

- the same as interest rate; the term 'discount' does not refer to the meaning of the word, but to the purpose of using the quantity, such as computations of present value, e.g. net present value or discounted cash flow

- the annual effective _____, which is the annual interest divided by the capital including that interest; this rate is lower than the interest rate; it corresponds to using the value after a year as the nominal value, and seeing the initial value as the nominal value minus a discount; it is used for Treasury Bills and similar financial instruments

The annual effective _____ is the annual interest divided by the capital including that interest, which is the interest rate divided by 100% plus the interest rate. It is the annual discount factor to be applied to the future cash flow, to find the discount, subtracted from a future value to find the value one year earlier.

For example, suppose there is a government bond that sells for $95 and pays $100 in a year's time.

a. Perpetuity
b. Discount rate
c. Stochastic volatility
d. Johansen test

24. A _____ is an expression that compares quantities relative to each other. The most common examples involve two quantities, but any number of quantities can be compared. _____s are represented mathematically by separating each quantity with a colon, for example the _____ 2:3, which is read as the _____ 'two to three'.
   a. 130-30 fund
   b. Y-intercept
   c. 100-year flood
   d. Ratio

25. _____ is a form of economic analysis that compares the relative expenditure (costs) and outcomes (effects) of two or more courses of action. _____ is often used where a full cost-benefit analysis is inappropriate e.g. the problem is to determine how best to comply with a legal requirement. Typically the CEA is expressed in terms of a ratio where the denominator is a gain in health from a measure (years of life, premature births averted, sight-years gained) and the numerator is the cost of the health gain.
   a. Cost-effectiveness analysis
   b. Benefit incidence
   c. Central limit order book
   d. Merchant capitalism

26.

The net present value (NPV) of all of a company's customers in terms of customer loyalty and indirectly, the revenue that the company can obtain from them. _____ is the total of the discounted lifetime values of all of the firm's customers.

In deciding the value of a company, it is important to know of how much value its customer base is in terms of future revenues.

a. Customer equity
b. Temporary equilibrium method
c. Marginal revenue
d. Product proliferation

Chapter 1
1. d   2. c   3. b   4. d   5. d   6. d   7. b   8. d   9. d   10. b
11. d   12. a   13. b   14. c   15. a   16. d   17. c   18. d   19. d   20. a

Chapter 2
1. d   2. d   3. c   4. d   5. d   6. a   7. d   8. a   9. d   10. a
11. d   12. d   13. d   14. c   15. a   16. d   17. c   18. d   19. d   20. d
21. c   22. c   23. d   24. b   25. d   26. b   27. d   28. d   29. b   30. d
31. d   32. d   33. d   34. a   35. d   36. b   37. a

Chapter 3
1. c   2. a   3. d   4. b   5. d   6. d   7. c   8. c   9. d   10. d
11. d   12. d   13. c   14. d   15. d   16. d   17. c

Chapter 4
1. d   2. d   3. a   4. c   5. c   6. d   7. a   8. d   9. a   10. d
11. c   12. d   13. a   14. d

Chapter 5
1. b   2. d   3. b   4. a   5. a   6. d   7. d   8. c   9. b   10. d
11. d   12. c   13. d   14. a   15. d   16. b   17. c

Chapter 6
1. b   2. d   3. d   4. a   5. d   6. b   7. d   8. d   9. d   10. b
11. c   12. c   13. d   14. d   15. c   16. a   17. b   18. d   19. d   20. d
21. d   22. d   23. b   24. b   25. d   26. d   27. d   28. d   29. d   30. d
31. b   32. b   33. d   34. d   35. b   36. d   37. b   38. a   39. b   40. d
41. a   42. d   43. d

Chapter 7
1. d   2. c   3. a   4. b   5. d   6. a   7. d   8. a   9. b   10. b
11. b   12. a   13. a   14. c   15. d   16. a   17. d   18. d   19. c   20. d
21. d   22. d   23. d

Chapter 8
1. d   2. d   3. d   4. a   5. b   6. d   7. a   8. b   9. d   10. a
11. b   12. d   13. d   14. b   15. d   16. d   17. d   18. c   19. d   20. b
21. d

Chapter 9
1. d   2. b   3. a   4. a   5. b   6. d   7. b   8. d

Chapter 10
1. d   2. d   3. d   4. d   5. c   6. d   7. b   8. d   9. d   10. c
11. b   12. b   13. a   14. d   15. b   16. d   17. b   18. d   19. d   20. a
21. b

ANSWER KEY

Chapter 11
    1. a   2. d   3. d   4. c   5. d   6. c   7. d   8. d   9. d   10. d
    11. c   12. d   13. d   14. c   15. d   16. d   17. d   18. d   19. d   20. d
    21. b   22. d

Chapter 12
    1. d   2. c   3. d   4. b   5. c   6. d   7. d   8. b   9. d   10. d
    11. d   12. b   13. b   14. d

Chapter 13
    1. d   2. b   3. d   4. b   5. d   6. d   7. d   8. c   9. d   10. d
    11. c   12. c   13. a   14. b   15. a   16. c   17. b   18. c   19. d   20. b
    21. c   22. b   23. a   24. d

Chapter 14
    1. a   2. d   3. d   4. c   5. c   6. c   7. d   8. b   9. b   10. d
    11. a   12. d   13. d   14. a   15. d   16. d   17. a   18. a   19. b   20. d
    21. c

Chapter 15
    1. a   2. d   3. c   4. b   5. d   6. c   7. d   8. d   9. a   10. d
    11. a   12. a   13. d   14. a   15. d   16. d   17. d   18. d   19. b   20. d
    21. d   22. d   23. d   24. d   25. d

Chapter 16
    1. d   2. a   3. d   4. d   5. b   6. b   7. c   8. a   9. d   10. d
    11. b   12. b   13. a   14. d   15. c   16. d   17. d   18. a   19. d   20. a
    21. a   22. b   23. a   24. d   25. d   26. d

Chapter 17
    1. d   2. c   3. d   4. d   5. d   6. a   7. c   8. d   9. a   10. d
    11. d   12. d   13. d   14. d   15. d   16. b   17. d   18. a   19. c   20. d
    21. b   22. d   23. b   24. d   25. a   26. a